DEATH
AND THE
AFTERLIFE

———————

DEATH
AND THE
AFTERLIFE

BRIAN INNES

ST. MARTIN'S PRESS
NEW YORK

DEATH AND THE AFTERLIFE

Copyright © 1999 by Brown Partworks

St. Martin's Press, Scholarly and Reference Division, 175 Fifth Avenue, New York, N.Y. 10010

First published in the United States of America in 1999

Printed in Dubai

ISBN: 0-312-22705-1

Library of Congress Cataloging-in-Publication Data

Innes, Brian.
    Death and the afterlife / Brian Innes.
        p.   cm.
    Includes bibliographical references and index.
    ISBN 0-312-22705-1 (cloth)
    1. Future life.   2. Death.   I. Title.
  BL535.I56   1999
  306.9—DC21   99-31476
                                         CIP

For Brown Partworks Ltd:
Managing Editor: Dawn Titmus
Project Editor: Julian Flanders
Design: Simon Wilder
Picture Research: Brigitte Arora
Production: Alex MacKenzie

C O N

T E N T S

'...An Awfully Big Adventure'

*ABOVE: **The Dance of Death became a popular image during the 14th and 15th centuries when the Black Death was rife.***
*RIGHT: **Fra Angelico's view of the torments of the lost souls in Hell.***

Death has rightly been called 'the final mystery'. Whatever our beliefs, whatever we may learn from the experiences of others, we will not know what death entails until that final moment when the last breath leaves our body. In the pathetic words of Peter Pan in J.M. Barrie's play, 'To die will be an awfully big adventure.'

There are some people who will say, boldly, that they are almost impatient for death, to discover what lies beyond. Usually, they will maintain this position while they are in good health and when the prospect of a natural death is still nothing more than a distant shadow on the horizon. Face them with a sudden, imminent demise, however, and they will fight to escape it like most other people – in fact, it might be argued that their continuing state of health somehow reflects an internal, unconscious struggle against death. The philosopher Jean-Jacques Rousseau (1712–78) wrote, 'He who pretends to look upon death without fear lies. All men are afraid of dying, this is the great law of sentient beings, without which the entire human species would soon be destroyed.'

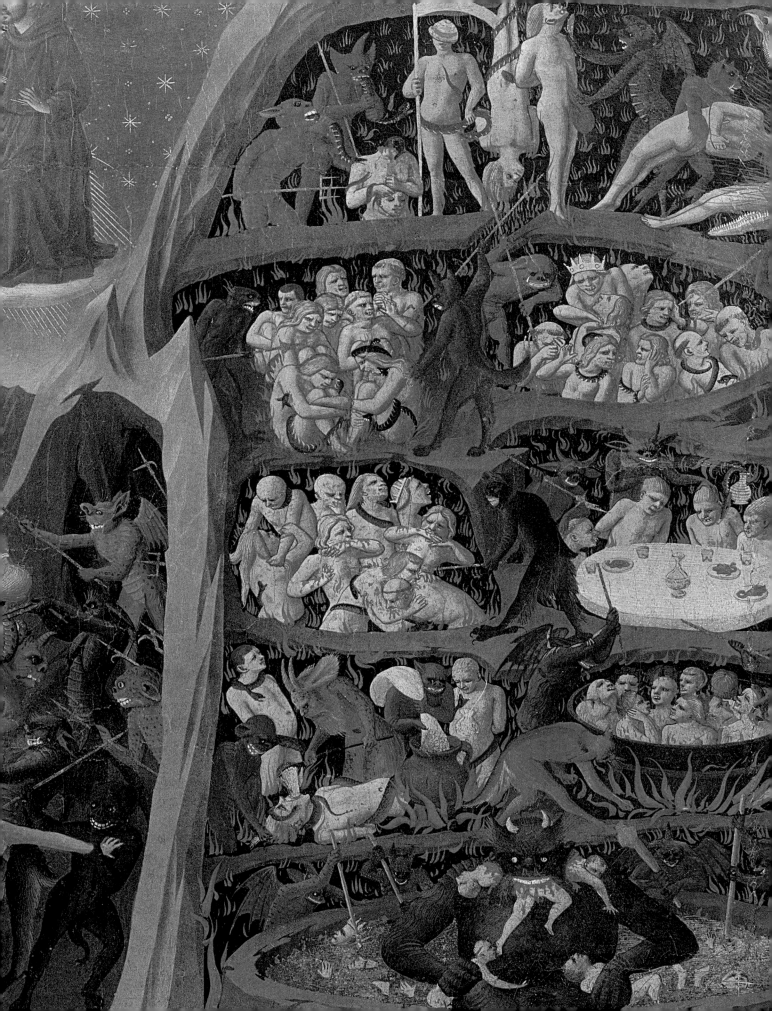

All the same, it is difficult even to define death. What might seem a simple matter has, with modern advances in medical techniques, become a labyrinth of ethics (see Chapter 1). And this is a question only of the physical body. It may have decayed or been consumed in the fire, leaving nothing but crumbling bones and a number of simple chemicals, but is that the end? All cultures throughout history have expressed belief in the survival after death of something other than the corporeal – a ghost, a spirit, a soul, a sentient existence of some sort.

Fear of death can be fear of the pains that must be suffered in the last moments of life, but it is also fear of what may follow. Shakespeare's Hamlet, pondering suicide, expressed his deep concern:

'Now get you to my lady's chamber, and let her paint an inch thick, to this favour she must come'. Laurence Olivier addresses the skull of Yorick, the court jester, in **Hamlet.**

To die, to sleep.
To sleep – perchance to dream, ay, there's the rub –
For in that sleep of death what dreams may come,
When we have shuffled off this mortal coil,
Must give us pause…
Who would fardels bear,
To grunt and sweat under a weary life,
But that the dread of something after death,
The undiscover'd country from whose bourn
No traveller returns, puzzles the will,
And makes us rather bear those ills we have,
Than fly to others that we know not of?

Hamlet, Act III, scene I

But what, in the gradual development of human belief in an afterlife, came first? Did a naked fear of the unknown have to be given justification in the concept of punishment of sins, or was it the expectation of judgment to come that engendered the fear? Certainly, all major religions express the belief that the actions of the living, good and bad, will be assessed after death and that they will determine what happens next – whether it will be admission to an eternal paradise, a return to a higher or a lower earthly existence by being reincarnated or a temporary or perpetual punishment in the agonies of Hell.

The ancient Sumerians appear to have believed that the sole purpose of humankind was to serve the gods by building temples and providing food for them; after

death they could no longer fulfil this function, so there was no reason for further existence and no possibility of punishment or reward. Yet even the Sumerians believed in a form of afterlife: their dead remained for ever as ghosts in a dark and comfortless limbo – a good enough reason for fear.

There are those who deny all religious beliefs, but even they fear death. It was the French philosopher Joseph Renan (1823–90) who prayed, 'O Lord, if there is a Lord, save my soul, if there is a soul.'

The ancient Greeks feared death so much that they preferred not to name it. Even today, a euphemism – a word that comes direct from the Greek, meaning 'use of good words' – frequently replaces the dreaded word 'died'. Many people avoid referring to the subject in any way. Grave inscriptions speak of someone having 'gone to sleep' or 'joined the angels'. Somehow, this softens the realisation of the harsh and unavoidable fact.

It was somewhat different in medieval times. Plague would suddenly break out and destroy whole communities; sporadic warfare could spawn marauding bands of soldiers who killed indiscriminately wherever they roamed. Sudden death became so familiar that whole populations were forced to accept it as a common event. As a result,

The Black Death epidemic struck Europe in 1347, spreading inland from the Mediterranean ports. This engraving depicts the scene in Florence, as described by Giovanni Boccaccio (1313–75).

9

The 'Divine Comedy', a long poem by Dante Alighieri (1265–1321), described his vision of Heaven and Hell. In the background of this fifteenth-century portrayal by Domenico di Miche-lino, the dead can be seen climbing up to Heaven, or descending into Hell.

pictorial representations of death, known as *memento mori* – decaying corpses, skulls and bones, a skeleton with a scythe (the 'grim reaper'), hourglasses and other images – appeared everywhere, on tombs, in manuscript illustrations and in woodcuts and paintings.

The most disastrous epidemic of plague in the history of the world – the 'Black Death' – began in Europe in 1347. It came from the east, where it had already ravaged China and Turkistan. It struck the army of Khan Janibeg as he besieged the trading port of Kaffa (later Feodosiya) in the Crimea, and he catapulted infected corpses into the town. Ships carried the disease to Mediterranean ports and it rapidly spread inland. So many people died within the next four years that the population of Europe did not return to its 1347 level until the sixteenth century. It was during this period that images of the 'dance of Death' became almost a popular art form. For a time, people were able to face the fact of death with a degree of resignation.

Nevertheless, it was in the two or three centuries following the Black Death that the first successful investigations were made into ways of saving and prolonging life. The Swiss physician Phillipus Aureolus Theophrastus Bombastus von Hohenheim (1493–1541), who called himself Paracelsus, has been described as the founder of modern medicine, 'the precursor of microchemistry, antisepsis, modern wound surgery, homeopathy, and a number of other ultra-modern achievements'. And this was also the time when the alchemists devoted their days, and their nights, to the search for the elixir of eternal life.

What may be considered the resentment of death developed during the nineteenth century. Medical science made so many advances at this time, so many were saved in circumstances from which, previously, they most certainly would have died, that people began to ask themselves whether death was inevitable. Early science fiction described the 'undead', vampires who lived for ever on the life-blood of others, and monstrous beings reconstructed from the spare parts of corpses. Scientists wondered why the body eventually ran down, why a mechanism that seemed to operate so efficiently should suddenly stop, and began to examine its physiological functions. Out of these early investigations have grown modern resuscitation techniques, organ replacement, genetic modification and cloning – and even the current preoccupation with cryonics, preserving the body for possible revival in the future.

The nineteenth century also saw the development of spiritualism and a growing belief that not only did the human personality survive, entire and unchanged, after death, but that it was possible to continue to communicate with those who had 'passed over'. People had always believed in ghosts, 'lost souls' who were condemned to wander without rest, but spiritualism opened up a novel concept: a community of spirits in a new, higher level of existence that was not to be confused with the Heaven or Hell of popular imagination.

But, for all this, we still have not lost our fear, and have found no way of defeating death. It comes in the end for everyone. As John Donne (1571–1631) wrote:

Any man's death diminishes me, because I am involved in Mankind;
And therefore never send to know for whom the bell tolls;
It tolls for thee.

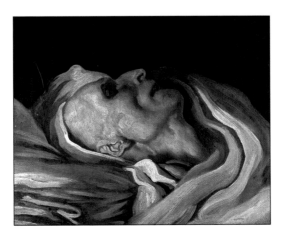

The end to which we must all come, when the last breath leaves our body. The French painter Théodore Géricault painted this picture of a dead man in 1818–19.

CHAPTER 1

'The Bourn from which No Traveller Returns'

What do we mean by death? Since, in its common usage, the word signifies 'cessation of life', any attempt to define death implies a definition of life. And this, as philosophers, biologists and divines have long known, is a far from simple matter.

At the lowest level of living organisms, the single cells of many bacteria can be dehydrated at low temperatures and reduced to a dry powder. In such a state they are, to all appearances, dead, and can remain so for perhaps hundreds of years. But given the development of suitable environmental conditions, they can return to a state in which they are able to perform all their normal metabolic functions. More than this, they are again able to divide and multiply.

Other unicellular organisms, such as the seeds of plants and the spores of fungi, behave similarly. Provided the molecular components

The human body is not immortal, a fact that carvers of funerary monuments have long recognized, but more primitive life forms can maintain a continuing existence.
FACING PAGE: *Detail from a tomb in Santa Maria del Popolo, Rome.*
LEFT: *Live spores released from a fungus can survive, apparently lifeless, for many years.*

of the cell remain unchanged, they are able to reproduce once more when conditions become favourable. Somehow, somewhere within the seemingly dead cell, there remains a 'principle of life'. But what this principle of life is, nobody can explain.

For such relatively simple life forms, then, death would appear to be no more than the loss of the ability to replicate. Higher up the scale, in multicellular organisms in which individual structures have specific functions, death can be defined as the cessation of metabolic processes. But this book is concerned with the death of far more complex organisms, and principally with that of human beings. Here, the problem of defining death has, particularly in recent times, become acute.

For many thousands of years, people had little doubt (and this still remains true among the more primitive cultures) when a person could be pronounced dead. Death occurred when he or she no longer breathed and when the heartbeat ceased. But the development of medical science has made this simple diagnosis invalid. Respiration can be restored, and the heart that has stopped can be started again. Modern medical literature is full of cases of people who 'died', but were subsequently resuscitated and returned to a full and active life.

The essential for human survival – and that of all higher forms of animal life – is a regular supply of oxygen. Without this, the body's cells can no longer generate energy and they progressively die. Writing in 1930, the British physiologist J.B.S. Haldane pointed out that oxygen deprivation 'not only stopped the machine, but wrecked the machinery'. Normally, oxygen is taken in from the air by the lungs, transferred to the blood and pumped round the body by the heart. These processes are dependent on one another, and if the lungs and heart cease working, death is imminent. Modern resuscitation techniques are directed at getting the machinery working again. If this is not possible, the patient can be put on a ventilator and external equipment used to keep the blood circulating.

SUSPENDED ANIMATION

In some cases, however, blood circulation and respiration may continue naturally, but at a very low level. This state of near-death is commonly called 'suspended animation'. It can be the result of severe shock following an accident, electrocution, or poisoning by barbiturates or narcotic drugs. Even qualified physicians can be deceived by the condition.

One morning in October 1969, for instance, the body of a young woman was found on a beach near Liverpool, England. The police immediately summoned a local doctor, who examined the body. Although the body was still warm, he failed to discover any other signs of life and pronounced the woman dead. A pathologist arrived shortly afterwards and agreed with the doctor's diagnosis.

The woman's body was taken to the mortuary. Three hours later, just as an autopsy was about to begin, a technician noticed that the woman's right eyelid was flickering and that a tear was forming. She was immediately covered and taken to an intensive-care unit, where she remained critically ill for several hours before her condition improved dramatically. Later hospital staff discovered that the young woman had taken an overdose of a barbiturate. She was transferred to a local psychiatric unit as a

Long before the English anatomist William Harvey (1578–1657) discovered the circulation system of blood, the Greeks, and others, recognized the cessation of the heartbeat as a sure sign of death.

voluntary patient. A week later, she discharged herself, apparently completely recovered.

Practitioners of yoga have claimed to be able to attain, voluntarily, a comparable state of suspended animation. This is *samadhi*, the eighth and final stage of hatha yoga. Stories abound of Tibetan monks who can spend weeks meditating in the eternal snows of the Himalayas, but few have been substantiated.

However, a remarkable case of *samadhi* was recorded in Lahore in 1838. It was witnessed by the distinguished Sikh leader, Maharajah Ranjit Singh, the British general Sir Claude Wade and several other British officers.

In front of the observers, a local yogi sat cross-legged on a white cloth and went into trance. A short time later, the corners of the cloth were tied over his head, and his stiffened body was lowered into a box, which was then padlocked and buried in a pit inside a garden pavilion. The doors of the pavilion were locked, and soldiers stood outside on 24-hour guard.

Thirty days later, the box was dug out, intact, in the presence of the maharajah, General Wade and a Dr McGregor. The man's body was apparently lifeless but, after his assistant had massaged him lightly, he recovered consciousness and, two hours later, was able to sit up and speak.

The man in this case was a local magician who made a living by performing acts of this kind. The case is reminiscent of some of the tricks carried out, although on a much smaller scale, by the American escapologist Harry Houdini. Nevertheless, the witnesses were convinced by the demonstration. Modern medical authorities, too, generally accept that suspended animation of this kind is possible. Some researchers have also pointed out the close similarity between certain forms of *samadhi* and the experiences of users of drugs such as LSD.

Because of the unreliability of the standard criteria – lack of detectable respiration and heart-

IN SOME CASES BLOOD CIRCULATION AND RESPIRATION CAN CONTINUE NATURALLY, BUT AT A VERY LOW LEVEL. THIS STATE OF NEAR-DEATH IS COMMONLY CALLED 'SUSPENDED ANIMATION'

beat – to establish death in cases of suspended animation, it is now customary to make use of electroencephalography (EEG). This measures the electrical activity of the brain. Although the heart may have stopped beating entirely, the brain can remain alive without it for up to 10 minutes, although gradual neurological damage will occur during this time.

But even EEG readings cannot be relied upon entirely. The absence of any electrical activity – a state sometimes called 'brain death' – can continue for some considerable time, sometimes up to 11 hours, if the heartbeat can be restored.

One typical case is of an elderly woman who had taken an overdose of sodium barbitone. On admission to hospital, she did not respond to any stimulus and there was no EEG activity. After eight hours, her brain showed slight activity, although there was no physical response to stimuli. The EEG activity gradually increased, and one month later, it was back to normal.

The term 'brain death' does not imply death of the cortical areas of the brain – those areas

Practitioners of yoga, like these young Buddhist monks, claim to be able to achieve a state of suspended animation.

RIGHT: *Intensive care in hospital can frequently restore a patient to life who would otherwise be given up for dead. This near-comatose man is attached to a ventilator, and a cardiac monitor detects the beating of his heart.*

that are principally concerned with sensory perception. It refers to those parts of the brain stem that control breathing, circulation and blood pressure – what are known as 'vital centres'. True brain death occurs only when these vital centres irreversibly cease to function.

Another near-death state, somewhat similar to suspended animation, is coma. This can be due to a number of causes – to chemical imbalance within the body, as in the case of diabetics, for example – but is most often due to brain damage, either from a physical accident or because of the rupture of blood vessels within the brain, commonly called a 'stroke'.

Frequently the damage is only partial, resulting in the loss of certain physical or mental functions but only partly affecting the 'vital functions' of heartbeat and respiration and the metabolic processes of the body. There are many cases of 'living vegetables' – people who remain alive, clinically, but who show very little EEG activity and do not respond to any stimuli.

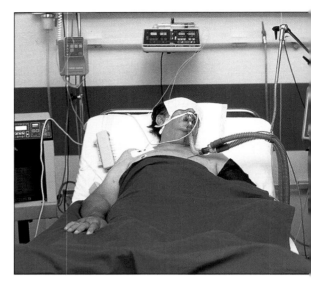

DEFINING BRAIN DEATH

In 1958 French neurologists described a condition that they called *coma dépassé* ('beyond coma'). The patients in this condition had irremediable brain damage and could be kept alive only on a ventilator. They not only made no response to external stimuli, but also they were unable to control their body temperature or

blood pressure; they could not retain water and passed large volumes of urine. The neurologists regarded this condition as a 'frontier state' between life and death. Usually, after a few days, the heartbeat ceased.

Ten years later, in 1968, an ad hoc committee of Harvard Medical School published a paper entitled 'A Definition of Irreversible Coma'. The paper listed criteria for recognition of brain death: the patient should be unable to breathe without a ventilator, should show no reflex response from the brain stem or spine and exhibit no EEG activity over a period of 24 hours. If these criteria were met, the ventilator could be disconnected and the patient could be pronounced dead.

Some time later, the Conference of Royal Colleges and Faculties of the United Kingdom published two memoranda, one in 1976 and the second in 1979. The first defined the clinical features of death of the brain stem, and the second equated death of the brain stem with clinical death.

In the United States, a report entitled 'Defining Death' was published by the President's Commission for the Study of Ethical Problems in Medicine and Biomedical and Behavioral Research in 1981. This included criteria very similar to those previously proposed. The commission put forward a model for a Uniform Determination of Death Act.

This model was subsequently endorsed by the American Medical Association, the

BELOW: *Modern technology makes it possible to scan the human brain and its activity, producing colourful images of this kind. 'Brain death' is now the only acceptable definition of final mortality.*

fmol/mgP
15.3
49.5
73.1
102.2
149.5
212.5
278.6

American Bar Association and the National Conference of Commissioners on Uniform State Laws. The statute has been adopted by most states of the Union, and similar criteria are widely accepted internationally.

LEGAL ASPECTS OF DEATH

The decision that a person has died can have very important legal implications. The determination of the time of death may be critical – in matters of inheritance, for example. A man's will may state that he leaves his estate to a specific heir, but in the event of that person's prior death, it is to go to others. If the two are pronounced dead at approximately the same time, it is essential to determine who died first. Questions concerning life insurance may also arise – for instance, when a renewal premium has not been paid, and the insurance expires on a given date.

So the death of a patient can place a heavy burden on a busy physician. In cases of unexpected death – and particularly when the body is discovered after some time, whether the result of an accident, suicide or even murder – the physician is required to give an estimate of the time of death. There is a succession of changes in the state of a dead body (see below), and these can be used to make an estimate of the time that has elapsed since death, but none is more than approximate.

With the development of organ transplantation techniques, further legal complications have ensued. Even after the vital centres have irreversibly ceased to function, many of the body's cells will remain alive for a limited time.

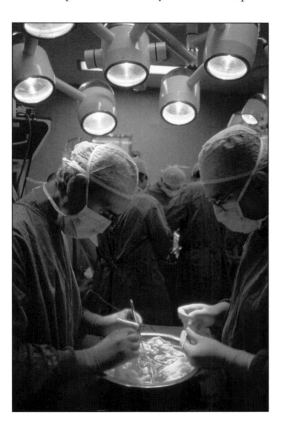

If an organ is to be removed from a patient's body and transplanted into another, it must be done as soon as possible. But who is to decide that the prospective organ donor is truly dead? After all, there might be a temptation to accelerate matters for the benefit of the recipient.

For example, the first heart transplant operation carried out at the Medical College of Virginia in Richmond, on 25 May 1968, resulted in a suit for medical malpractice. It transpired that the prospective donor had been kept alive by artificial respiration. The ventilator was switched off, and five minutes later, the patient was pronounced dead, so that the transplant could be made as soon afterward as possible.

Apart from the body organs, individual tissues can be kept alive and used in transplants. In September 1998 doctors in Lyon, France, reported that they had successfully transplanted a new hand on to the amputated stump of an Australian, who had lost his own hand in a chainsaw accident nearly 10 years before.

Ova and sperm also remain alive after clinical death and can be preserved. Also in 1998, in England, Mrs Diane Blood, a widow, wished to receive artificial insemination from the sperm of her deceased husband. It was refused, on the grounds that he had not given his express permission, and she had to carry her case to the highest court before her wish was granted. She later gave birth to a baby boy.

A transplant cannot be made without permission. Either the donor should have given clear written instructions, while still alive, that organs can be removed, or permission must be obtained from relatives and, in certain cases, from

The transplantation of human organs has raised many ethical questions about when a potential donor can be considered clinically dead.

the coroner if an inquest is to be held. Clearly, this can result in further legal complications.

The moment of death, the irreversible cessation of the vital functions, is known medically as somatic death. However, although oxygen is no longer being supplied to the body's cells, a variety of metabolic processes continue for some time – a condition described as molecular death.

THE PROGRESS OF DEATH

Since the blood is no longer being pumped around the body, its movement slows very rapidly. It gradually accumulates in the lower parts of the body, depending on the body's position, and gives a reddish-purple colour to the skin. This condition is known as hypostasis, or post-mortem lividity. If a body is later moved, hypostasis will indicate its original position.

Because the cells are no longer generating energy, the body's temperature begins to fall. One of the longest-established methods for estimating the time elapsed since death is to measure this temperature. It is, however, a somewhat inaccurate method. So many variables have to be taken into consideration: the temperature of the environment, the body's physique (an obese body cools more slowly than a slim one), the presence or absence of clothing or other covering and, indeed, the possibility that the person

died of hypothermia, so that the body had already cooled considerably before death.

The next obvious change in a dead body is the onset of rigor mortis. At first the body is flexible, but gradually the muscles stiffen because of chemical reactions. The muscles of the eyelids, face, lower jaw and neck stiffen to begin with, and then those of the trunk and limbs. This rigor generally begins about four hours after death and is complete within six. Then, as degeneration of the muscle fibres continues, rigor mortis passes after some 36 hours. As with the body temperature, the time of onset of rigor, and its passing, can be influenced by certain external conditions.

Interestingly, very high temperatures, such as those generated in a fire, can cause the muscles to contract and stiffen almost immediately. Fire victims are often found with their fists clenched and arms raised in front of the body (the 'pugilist posture') and with their knees drawn up.

Very occasionally – but generally only in conditions of extreme emotion or violence – instantaneous rigor mortis occurs. There is the story of a soldier whose body stayed mounted on his horse after he had been killed by a shell during the battle of Balaclava during the Crimean War. Similarly, at the defence of Sedan during the Franco-Prussian War in 1870, the

BELOW LEFT: Intense heat, as in a fire, can cause the dying body's muscles to stiffen and contract immediately. Fire victims, like this body from the ashes of Pompeii, are often found in the 'pugilist position' – fists clenched with knees drawn up.

BELOW RIGHT: It is often erroneously believed that a dead body will be destroyed by quick-lime. In fact, the lime acts as a preservative. The body of a North Vietnamese soldier killed in action, 1969.

FACING PAGE: Although the softer tissues rapidly decay after death, the bones of the skeleton – depending upon conditions – may remain unchanged for centuries. This skeleton was one of many discovered in Trondheim Cathedral, Norway.

body of a soldier, decapitated by a shell, remained rigid in a sitting position with his hand firmly holding a cup.

The body's muscles may remain active for some time (every medical student learns how the heart of a dissected frog can be kept beating by electrical stimulation), but from the moment of death, the body begins to putrefy. The process begins almost immediately in the dead cells, but the effects are not normally visible for two or three days. The decay is partly due to enzyme activity within the cells, but the principal cause is bacteria. For the most part, the bacteria come from the intestines and invade the tissues, but they can also come from the environment in which the body lies.

AS A GENERAL RULE, A BODY EXPOSED TO AIR WILL DECOMPOSE TWICE AS FAST AS ONE IN WATER, AND FOUR TIMES AS FAST AS ONE BURIED IN THE GROUND

The first signs of decay generally appear in the skin of the lower right abdomen, as bacteria from the gut decompose the haemoglobin of the blood into greenish compounds. Then the veins on the thighs and shoulders become outlined in red or green as the bacteria proliferate, and, after about a week, the whole body will have taken on a characteristic 'marbled' appearance.

The next phase is the formation of gas in the body cavities and the appearance of large blisters on the skin, which then begins to peel off. The gas causes the tongue and eyes to protrude, and body fluids are squeezed out of the mouth, nostrils and other orifices.

This stage can sometimes occur much earlier, and on one occasion, caused a highly respectable man to be suspected of murder. It was known that he had quarrelled with his wife and had stormed from the house. The following day, her body was found in bed with blood-stained fluid oozing from her mouth. At first it was assumed that her husband had killed her. Her death was eventually discovered to be due to a massive barbiturate overdose, and it turned out that, during 24 hours of a very hot summer, her body had already reached this relatively advanced stage of putrefaction.

If the body is left exposed, flies will lay eggs in any available opening, and maggots will develop and subsequently pupate. This can provide some further indication of the time that has elapsed since death.

The rate of putrefaction depends upon external conditions, but within weeks the tissues will liquefy, although organs such as the uterus or glands such as the prostate may remain relatively unchanged for many months. As a general rule, a body exposed to air will decompose twice as fast as one in water, and four times as fast as one buried in the ground.

After several months, but sometimes as little as three weeks, a dead body, when totally submerged in water – but sometimes just in wet surroundings – can develop adipocere. This is a greyish, soapy substance produced by chemical changes in the body fat. In people with a considerable quantity of subcutaneous fat, this adipocere can preserve the shape of the original body, so that the face remains recognisable even after many years. On the other hand, a body left in warm, dry surroundings can become mummified. This natural mummification can be complete within months and persist for many years, and identifiable physical features are preserved. Tiny stillborn babies hidden by their mothers or babies that are killed deliberately after birth often mummify because of the absence of bacteria in their bodies.

Eventually, most bodies are reduced to skeletons as the decayed tissues are consumed by many different agents. In temperate zones, most of the soft tissue will have disappeared after one to two years, but the tendons, ligaments, hair and nails may survive much longer. The bones remain solid for many years, and pathologists are able to make an estimate of the deceased's age and sex. After 40 to 50 years, however, they begin to become dry and brittle and are gradually of little more than archaeological interest.

LOOKING AT DEATH

The human race has a whole spectrum of attitudes to death. At one extreme there are those who confess to being terrified of the very idea of death, and refuse to discuss the subject or consider it in any way, whether in reference to themselves or anybody else. At the other are those who not only accept death as a natural end to life, but are almost impatient to discover what lies beyond it. In between lie many other attitudes: from those who still regard death as fearful and a cause of almost insupportable grief; those who can accept the death of others but somehow consider themselves immune; those who realise that death is inevitable and resign themselves – although often with considerable resentment – to what is to come; those who believe that death is a time for celebrating the life that has passed; to those who, like the poet John Keats, are 'half in love with easeful Death'.

All these attitudes presuppose (as did Keats) a peaceful, painless death. In modern Western society, steps are taken to shield survivors from any contact with the distressing aspects of death. The closed coffin distances mourners from the deceased, leaving them only with their memories; the open coffin presents a corpse that has received the expert attention of embalmers and cosmeticists. In many countries, the dead body no longer remains in the parlour at home before the burial. The parlour has become the 'living room', and the body is removed to the funeral *parlour* at the funeral *home*.

It is, perhaps, this normal distancing from death that draws a crowd to the scene of a fatal accident. In his book *Disaster* (1974), Allen Troy wrote, 'the variety of motives that make up this impulse to gather at the scene of a disaster cover a range that perhaps begins with a desire for a vicarious taste of violence at a crushed body or a severed limb, and extends into enthusiastic self-congratulations of having missed the consequences of disaster oneself.'

The occasion of violent death often provokes a primitive reaction. Over 100,000 people travelled a considerable distance just to stare at a field outside Paris, where the serial murderer Jean-Baptiste Troppmann had killed and buried seven of his eight victims in 1869. Thousands took the train to Palmetto, Georgia, in 1899 to see a black man lynched and buy a slice of his body as a souvenir. And when 'Public Enemy No.1' John Dillinger was gunned down by G-men outside the Biograph cinema in Chicago in 1934, hundreds of bystanders dipped their dresses, handkerchiefs and scraps of paper in his blood to mark the occasion.

Death, in all its forms, has a gruesome fascination for the living. In countries where public execution is still carried out – here, the hanging of two convicted murderers in Lebanon in 1996 – the ceremony can draw huge crowds of spectators.

Elisabeth Kübler-Ross, the American psychiatrist whose definition of the five phases of the journey toward death has had a powerful influence on the treatment of terminally ill patients.

Age can affect one's attitude to death. Commenting on the drowning of a swimmer, *Miami Herald* reporter Edna Buchanan wrote in 1992:

Young people are drawn morbidly to death. They even carry babies and lead small children by the hand to come quick and see this awful something…

But the elderly won't go out of their way to see a dead body. They won't go out of their way to avoid one, either. Elderly bathers will slip surreptitiously under yellow police lines protecting a body in an alley and drag their beach chairs down that alleyway, carefully skirting the corpse, of course, simply because it is the most direct route to their destination. Why detour for death?

However, as Christine Quigley has written in *The Corpse: A History* (1996):

Time does not erase the fear and awe we have in the presence of death and its victims… We may look at a corpse to discern differences between it and us. If the body is that of a 70-year-old man or woman, the young may relax their guard a little, considering the death to be in the natural order of things. If the body belongs to a 20-year-old man who was struck by a car, or a 30-year-old woman stalked and killed by a serial murderer, the tables are turned with the realization that we have little control over death at best. Fear of the dead is now fear of the failings of contemporary medicine, but it has always been fear that we could be next.

THE PSYCHOLOGY OF DYING

As we have seen, people approach death in many different ways. In most cultures, death is generally a time for mourning: always for the loss of a loved one, and in the case of children and young people, for the fact that they have died

before they were able to fulfil the potential of their lives. But there are also social pressures: people are expected to mourn, and funeral rites are often designed to give the bereaved this opportunity (see Chapter 4).

But what of the dying person? Everybody hopes to make 'a good death', but this is not always possible. Until recently in the West – and still in most other parts of the world – most people died as quietly and contentedly as possible (given their physical condition), surrounded by their family and friends, with a priest present to administer the last rites. Tolstoy describes (in *The Death of Ivan Illich*, 1886) the death of an old coachman who remarks resignedly, 'Death is here, and that is how it is.'

However, the developments of modern medical science have changed all this. In very many cases, the condition has changed from that of a dying person to that of a dying patient. In *Confronting Death* (1996), David Wendell Moller wrote:

A modern person is identified as dying only when the disease has been objectively and clinically diagnosed. In addition to the medical diagnosis, a subjective label must accompany the medical determination. This entails the recognition by physicians and other health care providers that, in all likelihood, the progress of the disease will lead to the death of the patient. Obviously, a person comes to recognize that he is dying when he accepts the subjective label that originates from the medical diagnosis. Therefore, a person may not legitimately declare himself to be dying solely on the basis of personal judgment…

The process of care for a dying patient has been given the name of 'thanatology' – from the Greek word *thanatos*, meaning 'death'. One of the most prominent figures in the study of thanatology has been the American psychiatrist Elisabeth Kübler-Ross. As a small child, she witnessed the dignified death of a local farmer who had fallen from a tree:

He asked simply to die at home, a wish that was granted without question…He arranged his affairs quietly, though he was in great pain…When he did die, he was left at home, in his beloved home which he had built, and amidst his friends and neighbors who went to take a last look at him where he lay in the midst of flowers in the place he had lived in and loved so much.

In her most famous book, *On Death and Dying* (1969), Kübler-Ross contrasted this homely death with what happens to so many hospital patients:

One of the most important facts is that dying nowadays is more gruesome in many ways, namely: lonely, mechanical and dehumanised; at times it is even difficult to determine technically when the time of death has occurred.

Dying becomes lonely and impersonal because the patient is often taken out of his familiar environment and rushed to an emergency room…

He may cry for rest, peace and dignity, but he will get infusions, transfusions, a heart machine, or tracheotomy if necessary. He may want one single person to stop for one single minute, so he can ask a single question – but he will get a dozen people round the clock, all busily preoccupied with heart rate, pulse, electrocardiogram or pulmonary functions, his secretions and excretions, but not with him as a human being…Is our concentration on equipment, on blood pressure, our desperate attempt to deny the impending death which is so frightening and discomforting to us that we displace all our knowledge onto machines, since they are less close to us than the suffering face of another human being which would remind us once more of our lack of omnipotence, our own limits and failures, and last but not least perhaps our own mortality?

By interviewing some 200 dying patients, Kübler-Ross identified five phases of the journey towards death. The first, a relatively temporary one, is denial. The second phase is anger, 'When the first stage of denial cannot be maintained any longer, it is replaced by feelings of anger, rage, envy and resentment.' She recognised that an angry patient presents problems, both for the family and for the medical staff,

and wrote that it was important to respect and understand the feelings of the patient.

The third phase Kübler-Ross identified as 'bargaining', an attempt to negotiate for more time. She compared this phase with the dishonest bargains that children frequently make with their parents. Kübler-Ross noted that, even if patients lived to the point they had bargained for, they were still not necessarily ready to accept death at that stage.

The fourth phase, said Kübler-Ross, was depression. She defined two types: reactive and preparatory. Reactive depression is a response to everything that is lost in the process of dying – self-image, possessions, financial situation and so on. Preparatory depression is due to the recognition of further impending loss. 'The patient is in the process of losing everything and everybody he loves. If he is allowed to express his sorrow, he will find final acceptance much easier.'

The final phase is acceptance:

There comes a time for the 'final rest before the long journey'…This is the time when the television is off. Our communications then become more nonverbal than verbal. The patient may just make a gesture of the hand to invite us to sit down for a while. He may just hold our hand and ask us to sit in silence…We may together listen to the song of a bird from the outside…It may reassure him that he is not left alone when he is no longer talking, and a pressure of the hand, a look, a leaning back in the pillows, may say more than many 'noisy' words.

The open expression of grief on the part of the bereaved is an important element in coming to terms with the fact of death. In his last phases, the patient, too, says Kübler-Ross, should be allowed to express his sorrow.

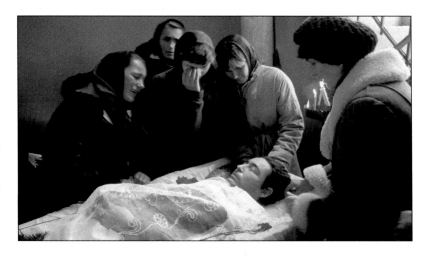

CHAPTER 2

MYTHS OF MORTALITY AND DEATH

From the earliest times human beings have puzzled over death. Why do people die? Is death an inevitable end to life or is it some kind of punishment? Different attempts at explanation are embodied in the myths that have developed on the subject all over the world.

'A myth', wrote British anthropologist Cottie Burland in *Myths of Life and Death* (1974), 'is a truth in an irrational form. It tells a story using pictures and thoughts in its own context; encapsulated truths, all the more palatable because of their disguises.' Myths are not only the folklore of primitive cultures; in one form or another, they survive even in the most sophisticated societies.

There are similarities between myths from widely separated cultures, but there are also striking differences. Most myths about the origin of death assume that humankind was originally created immortal, and death came as an intruder. But there are different reasons given for its arrival. In some myths it comes as the result of an error, a message misunderstood. In others, it is sent as a punishment for disobedience, ingratitude or stupidity (as in the Judaeo-Christian story of

Adam and Eve). And yet, in other myths, death is the result of an agreement, either between the gods or between the first men and women. Many of the stories seem to assume that, but for an unhappy accident, humans would have been able to renew their lives over and over again, like the moon in its phases – or the snake which, it was believed, achieved immortality each time it shed its skin.

AFRICAN MYTHS

The concept of death as a message that was wrongly delivered, or delivered too late, occurs in many African myths. There are several versions of the story of the chameleon who was sent by God to tell humankind that they could be immortal should they wish it. Unfortunately, the chameleon took his time and was overtaken on the way by a lizard, who was also carrying a message, but his message was that humans had to die when their time was up.

In East Africa a myth of the Galla people tells of a messenger bird who was sent by God to tell human beings that they could renew their

FACING PAGE: It was the sin of Adam and Eve in disobeying God's orders, says the Bible story, that brought death into the world. This painting by Lucas Cranach the Elder (1472–1553) depicts the critical moment when Eve persuaded Adam to eat the fruit of the Tree of Knowledge of Good and Evil.

ABOVE: Among many peoples, there is no written form of religious dogma, and the beliefs surrounding death must be transmitted from generation to generation by oral tradition. Here men of the Dinka people of the Sudan gather round one of the elders to listen to his storytelling.

ABOVE RIGHT: Death entered African mythology at a very early stage. This reliquary figure from Gabon was intended to protect its owner from death.

lives simply by changing their skins. But on the way he met a snake feeding on a dead animal. The bird was hungry, and offered to tell the snake 'God's news' in exchange for some of the meat. The snake agreed, and the bird told him that all he had to do to remain youthful was to cast off his skin, but that people would grow old and die. God was so angry that his message was not delivered properly that he gave the bird a pain in the belly, and to this day it flies from tree to tree, bleating *wakatia-a-a–a* – 'God help me'. Locally the bird is known as the *holwaka*, 'the sheep of God', and to ornithologists as the white-bellied go-away bird.

In a Hottentot myth from South Africa, it was the Moon who sent the message, via an insect. The insect was to tell humans that their lives would be renewed regularly, like the Moon itself. As the insect crawled slowly along, it met a hare, who asked where it was going and why. The hare said as he was so much quicker, he would carry the message. But in his haste he made a mistake and delivered the message incorrectly, reporting that, unlike the Moon, humankind was doomed to die for ever. And so it came to pass.

GOD WAS SO EXASPERATED THAT HE DECIDED IF HUMAN BEINGS WERE GOING TO KEEP THWARTING HIS ATTEMPTS TO SAVE THEM, HE WOULD LEAVE THEM TO IT

The immortality of the Moon is also the theme of a myth among the Upotos of the Congo. In the earliest days of the world, God summoned the inhabitants of both the Earth and the Moon to attend on him. The Moon-men obeyed at once, but the Earthmen dallied. In his anger, God rewarded the Moon-men with immortality but condemned the inhabitants of the Earth to die.

A legend of the Baganda people from southern Uganda, explaining that death was a penalty for disobedience, is reminiscent of the Greek myth of Orpheus and Eurydice, or even the Bible story of Lot and his wife. The first man on Earth, Kintu, was permitted to marry one of the daughters of Heaven, whose brother was Death. God sent the married pair to live on Earth, giving them a hen for food. He warned them on no account to stop or turn back, but to hurry in case they met Death on the way. But the woman forgot the hen's food and returned to Heaven for it, and Death saw her and followed the couple back to Earth.

Kintu appealed to God for help. God sent another of his sons, named Digger, to bring Death back. But Death hid in the ground and no one could find him. God imposed a spell of total silence while Digger listened for him. But the cries of Kintu's children broke the spell, and so Death escaped and to this day remains at large on Earth.

A very old story is still told by the people who live on the shores of Lake Kivu, on the borders of Rwanda and Zaire. God made humans immortal, but he had to keep a close eye on Death, who was forever trying to provoke men into a fight, which he always won.

One day, when God was away, Death killed an old woman, who was then buried. When God returned, he noticed that the old woman was missing. Death fled in fear of him. He met another old woman and persuaded her to hide him under her skirt, whereupon he entered her body. When God found her, he decided that, as she was old, it would be easiest to kill her and tear out Death. But Death slipped away, fled again and this time persuaded a young woman to hide him in her belly. God was so exasperated that he decided if human beings were going to keep thwarting his attempts to save them, he would leave them to it, so he let Death alone to do as he liked.

There are many West African stories about the spider Yiyi, and one of these explains the coming of Death. It was during a time of famine, but Death was not worried – he had plenty to eat because he set traps for animals in the forest. Yiyi, however, was hungry. He begged Death for a supply of meat and, in exchange, gave him his daughter in marriage. Death warned his new wife never to go near his traps when she went to fetch water. One day, however, she fell into one of the traps, and Death accidentally cut her up for his food.

When Yiyi learnt what had happened, he attacked Death with a knife. But Death was strong and Yiyi ran back to the village and hid, with Death pursuing him. Death had never been to the village before, and while he waited for Yiyi to appear, he amused himself by shooting at women as they went to the river to fetch water. It was then that he realised it was a waste of effort to set traps in the forest, when all the flesh he wanted was here in the village. So he stayed for ever.

NATIVE AMERICAN MYTHS

The spider stories of West Africa are often similar to the stories of the coyote – the 'Trickster' – of North America, but this mischievous creature plays a very different part in a myth of the Wintun, a small Native American tribe from the Pacific coast.

When God decided to create humankind, he ordered two buzzards, who were brothers, to erect a stone stairway between Earth and Heaven. At the top, there were to be two springs of water, one for purification and the other as a source of immortality. As the two brothers laboured away, Sedit the coyote came to mock them. Did they really think, he asked, that people would want to climb that long staircase, again and again, endlessly renewing their lives? 'Joy at birth and grief for the dead,' he said, 'are better, for these mean love.'

The coyote is one of the 'tricksters' of North American myth, but in several of the stories he was also held responsible for the coming of death.

Persuaded that their work was worthless, the brothers destroyed what they had built. But the younger brother then pointed out that it was only right that Sedit should take his own advice and accept death himself. But Sedit did not want to die and he made himself wings out of sunflower petals and tried frantically to fly to Heaven. But as he rose up into the sky the sun withered the petals and he fell to Earth. God told him that he was condemned by his own words and that because of his mischievousness, all humans were now fated to die.

Another coyote myth tells a very different story. Coyote was sad because his sister and friends had died and gone to the land of the spirits; and Eagle, too, was mourning the death of his wife. Together they set out for the land of the spirits to bring their loved ones back. When they got there, they found the spirits of their friends dancing and singing in the light of the

Coyote carrying the basket and Eagle flying overhead. But Coyote found the basket very heavy, and the spirits inside were complaining. Eventually Coyote said, 'We are far enough from the land of the spirits now. I'll let them out, and they won't go back.' But the spirits flew out like wind and returned to the land of the dead.

Eagle was angry at first, but then he said, 'It is autumn now, and the leaves are falling, just as people die. Let us try again in the spring.' But Coyote replied, 'I am too tired. Let the dead stay in the land of the dead forever.'

Among the Algonquin tribes, a similar story claims that immortality was granted by the Great Hare, who gave it to the first man in a little package, which he was forbidden to open. But his wife, unable to contain her curiosity, was tempted to look inside. As she opened the package, immortality flew out, never to return.

A very different myth occurs among the Tlingit of Alaska. The creator god was Raven, and he attempted to make men from rock, so that they would last for ever. But this proved unsuccessful, because it made them slow of movement. So Raven made them from leaves – quick and light, but condemned to die like plants.

FAR LEFT: In Native American belief, the spirits of animals were held to be as important as those of human beings. Here an Algonquin hunter blows tobacco smoke in the mouth of a bear he has just killed to make peace with its departed spirit.

Moon. Close to the Moon stood Frog, the master of the spirits. As dawn broke, the spirits left for their daily sleep. With no one else around, Coyote struck and killed Frog and dressed in his skin. Next evening, the spirits returned. When the festivities were at their height, Coyote swallowed the Moon, and in the darkness, Eagle captured the spirits, put them into Coyote's basket and closed the lid. Then the pair began their return to the land of the living,

LEFT: This woman belongs to the Inuit of Alaska who relate how an old woman declared that, if it was impossible to have sunlight without death, she would rather have both.

As in Irian Jaya, skulls are venerated in Papua New Guinea, where many similar myths have been recorded. Here, a woman holds what looks like the preserved head of her grandfather.

had magic powers: she turned the piece of bone into a stone and it sank.

A somewhat similar story is told by the Inuit of Alaska. In the beginning, it says, there was no death – but there was also no sun. One old woman announced that she could be happy without sunlight if it meant there was no death. But another declared that, if it was not possible to have one without the other, she would rather have both because life without light was too much to bear. So death exists as the darkness and life exists as light.

Much further south, around the Orinoco River in Venezuela, another old woman is similarly blamed for the loss of immortality. Once again, it seems that God intended that human beings should live forever by changing their skins, but an old lady laughed so much at the idea that God changed his mind.

PACIFIC AND AUSTRALIAN MYTHS

Far away from Venezuela, among the islands of Polynesia and westwards into Southeast Asia, the same myth about skin-changing can be found. One Polynesian myth recounts how everybody changed skins as they grew old, and returned to their youthful forms. But one day, a child cried because it could not recognise its newly rejuvenated mother. She was so upset that she put her old skin back on again, and since then, everyone has done the same.

In Papua and Irian Jaya, the protagonist of a similar myth is called Sido, a sort of pre-human entity. He had two mothers, who were joined together like Siamese twins until he separated them. In an attempt to avoid his death, he lay in a trench and shed his skin like a snake, but some children spied on him and he died. His mothers dug up his skull and cleaned it, and one or the other wore it around her neck. They followed his spirit as it wandered, but made the mistake of using the skull to give his spirit water to drink. As a result, he could never be reborn.

Another Irian Jaya myth, of a different kind, concerns an old man called Manarmakeri, who had a vision of immortality. He travelled widely, conferring his vision on all those who were kind

The concept of a debate about death is found in a Blackfoot myth, which describes how the first old man and the first old woman discussed what was to happen to them. The man desired immortality, but the woman said that this would mean the Earth becoming overcrowded. Besides, she said, only if people died would the survivors would be able to experience grief and sympathy for one another. The two agreed to look for a sign. They decided they would throw a piece of buffalo bone into the water to help them decide what to do. If it floated, they would choose immortality; if it sank, they would accept death. But the woman

In both Papua New Guinea and Irian Jaya myths describe how the skull of Sido, a pre-human entity, was the source of death. But this Irian Jayan man sleeps with a skull as his pillow to bring him good fortune.

enough to welcome him. But many people had no faith in his message because he was old and unkempt, and in rejecting it, they lost their chance of immortality.

The concept of death as a penalty for disobedience is found in a myth from one group of Aborigines of New South Wales, Australia. It was taboo for people to go near a particular hollow tree, in which bees were nesting. The men obeyed, but some of the women were anxious to get at the honey. Eventually, one woman took an axe and struck the tree. Death flew out in the shape of a bat, and now condemns all living things to die by touching them with its wings.

On the Admiralty Islands in the Pacific Ocean, the first man is said to have fled from Death and hidden within a tree. As a reward for hiding him, the tree asked for two white pigs. But the man brought one white pig and one black pig that he had disguised with chalk. The tree was so enraged that it said it would not protect the man from Death any longer.

THE CONCEPT OF DEATH AS A PENALTY FOR DISOBEDIENCE IS COMMON IN MYTHS FROM MANY DIFFERENT CULTURES

A very different story is told on the Indonesian island of Sulawesi. At one time, it says, the sky was quite close to the Earth, and God used to lower gifts down to the people on a rope. He sent down a stone, which they rejected, and then he lowered a banana, which, of course, they welcomed. As a result, God announced that human beings would not be immortal, like the stone, but as impermanent and perishable as the banana.

Among the Aranda Aborigines of Central Australia, the origin of death is attributed to an evil bird – the magpie Urbura. In the beginning, women and first and then men emerged from under the rocks. The chief among the men was hated and envied by the others because he had the first choice of women. They pointed a magic bone at him, so that he fell unconscious, and then they buried him. But he was not dead, and his head broke out of the ground. Urbura flew up, stabbed the man in the throat and ordered him to remain dead for ever, while all the others were turned into grieving birds.

*ABOVE: **The supreme trinity of Hindu gods, Vishnu, Shiva and Prajapati (later known as Brahma).***

A myth reminiscent of the story of Adam and Eve comes from the Indonesian island of Roti, where one of the principal crops is the lontar palm. On Roti, it is not an apple, but the sugary lontar fruit that brought death:

If you pick the fruit of the syrup tree
Or if you pluck the leaf of the honey tree
There is a sourness there
A spirit of death lies there…

It is for this reason that the lontar palm is cut down, and its wood used to make coffins.

HINDU MYTHS

The *Rig-Veda* is a mythology in the form of more than a thousand poems, written in Sanskrit about 2000 BC. It tells of a trinity of supreme gods, the *trimurti*: Vishnu, Shiva and Prajapati (later known as Brahma), who held the balance between the other two and came to be named 'Lord of Creatures'. He created four sons, Fire, Wind, the Sun and the Moon, and a daughter, the Dawn, whom he desired: 'She fled from him in the form of a doe, and so he became a stag; she became a cow, he a bull; she a mare, he a stallion; and this way all the species were created, even the ants.'

The principal offspring of Prajapati became gods or demons. They were in a constant struggle, one against the other. But the greatest enemy of the gods, and of Prajapati, was Death. In the

*FAR RIGHT: **The Sumerian goddess Inanna descended into the kingdom of death in search of her beloved Dumuzi. There she appeared naked before her sister Ereshkigal, but was then stripped of life itself.***

beginning, after he had conceived the gods and humankind, Prajapati created the god of Death. But Prajapati was not immortal: one half of him – mind, voice, breath, eye and ear – was, but the other half – hair, skin, flesh, bone and marrow – was mortal. So he fled in terror of the death he had created.

Eventually, he was made immortal through a sacrificial ritual, a ritual that Hindu priests were to search for over many centuries. Then the other gods gained their immortality through Prajapati, and from then Death was no longer their enemy. But the god of Death protested that he now had no function, and so the gods ordered that the human body should be his share. In this way, the gods assured their own immortality by condemning humankind to death.

SUMERIAN MYTHS

More than 6,000 years ago, the great goddess of the Sumerians in Mesopotamia was called Inanna – later known as Ishtar, or Astarte. She fell insatiably in love with, and then lost, the handsome Dumuzi. While searching for him, she descended into the kingdom of death, losing on the way all her jewels and clothing, until she appeared naked before her sister, Ereshkigal. And there she was stripped of life itself and her corpse was thrust on to a stake.

After three days, the messenger of true speech, Ninshubar, learnt what had happened and went to the house of the god Enlil, the father of Inanna, lamenting, 'Let not your daughter be destroyed in the depths! You would not allow jewels to be ground into powder, nor the precious wood for caskets to be made into laths by the woodworkers. Do not let your young daughter be dead in the underworld.' But Enlil replied that Inanna was the victim of her own lust, and now she had undergone the rituals of the underworld, she must accept death.

Ninshubar went to the house of Nanna, the Moon goddess, but she gave him the same answer. So he went to the house of the god Enki. The god wept at Ninshubar's news and agreed to help. He took the black dust from his fingernail and named it the food of life; he took the red lacquer from his fingernail and named it the water of life. Then he ordered messengers to descend into the underworld – 'buzzing like flies about the gates' – where they would find Ereshkigal in the pangs of childbirth.

She received them, and they were offered drink from the river of the dead, which they refused, and the food of the dead, which they likewise refused. They asked for only one thing – 'this rotting body'. 'It is your queen,' said Ereshkigal, 'and as this carrion was your queen, you may have it.' Then the messengers sprinkled the black and red powders from Enki's fingernails on the body, and Inanna stood up, alive, naked and beautiful once more.

However, the spirits of the underworld decided that Inanna could not leave unless she undertook to find a substitute to replace her. She searched through all the cities of the land until she found Dumuzi. She sent him to the underworld, while she flew up and took her proper place among the gods. This satisfied the underworld, but all the people wept for Dumuzi, and at last it was arranged that he should spend half the year below, and that for the other half of the year, his sister should go in place of him. Each year the women wept for Dumuzi and rejoiced at his return.

This myth is regarded as perhaps the earliest recorded expression of the idea of resurrection after death, which is in itself a reflection of the cycle of the seasons (see Chapter 6).

> 'YOU WOULD NOT ALLOW JEWELS TO BE GROUND INTO POWDER, NOR THE PRECIOUS WOOD FOR THE CASKETS TO BE MADE INTO LATHS BY THE WOODWORKERS. DO NOT LET YOUR DAUGHTER BE DEAD IN THE UNDERWORLD'

GRAECO-ROMAN MYTHS

Unlike other more primitive peoples, the Greeks, and later the Romans – who shared many of their religious beliefs – do not seem to have spent much time questioning the occurrence of death. They appear to have regarded it as a part of life – an inevitable end to it, but something ordained from the very beginning, something that people had learned to accept without question.

When the cosmos had been formed out of Chaos, it had to be peopled. The goddess Gaia, 'the deep-breasted Earth', united with her son, Uranus, and produced the first race of twelve Titans, who were the ancestors of humankind. The last-born of Gaia was Cronos, who, at his mother's instigation, castrated Uranus and became chief of the new dynasty. Under his rule, creation continued.

Night gave birth to all the troubles that afflict humans: Doom (Moros), Death (Thanatos), Nemesis and the three Fates: Clotho, Lachesis and Atropos. She also bore Fraud, Incontinence, Old Age and Strife, who in turn gave birth to Sorrow, Forgetfulness, Hunger, Disease, Combat, Murder, Battles, Massacres, Quarrels, Lies, Equivocations, Injustice and Oaths.

Euripides described Thanatos as walking among humankind, dressed in a black robe and carrying the sword of death. However, he was more often represented as a winged spirit, like his brother Hypnos (sleep), who dwelt with him in the underworld and put people to sleep by waving his wings above them.

Of the three Fates, Clotho was the spinner of a person's destiny, Lachesis wove the web of chance by which the person's life was maintained and Atropos finally cut the thread to end life. The agents of the Fates were the Keres. When the fatal hour came, they appeared in order to carry off the unhappy mortal to the underworld.

Similar to them were the Erinnyes, or Eumenides. Scholars disagree on the significance of the name 'Eumenides', which means 'the benevolent ones'. Some maintain that it refers to their mild treatment of Orestes after he had murdered his mother. Others believe that the Greeks preferred, superstitiously, not to refer to them by their proper name.

The particular mission of the Erinnyes was to punish those who murdered their parents or who violated their oaths. These black goddesses would appear on the threshold of the guilty person's house, their hair writhing with snakes, and it was impossible to escape them.

One way or another, the world of the Greeks was peopled with death.

The human skull – the 'death's head' – has been an emotive symbol for many centuries, as in this Roman mosaic, now in the national archaeological museum in Naples.

CHAPTER 3

UNNATURAL DEATH

Most people die naturally, as the body's mechanisms gradually fail, sometimes as the result of progressive disease. Others die unexpectedly, when the heart or lungs suddenly cease working for one reason or another, or there is a rupture of a blood vessel in the brain. Some are the victims of accidents, or even of murder. These are all involuntary deaths. However, the cause of death that has continued to puzzle both psychologists and philosophers is suicide.

Suicide is defined as the act of intentionally and voluntarily taking one's own life. There is no doubt about the intention, but how voluntary the act is can be affected by external pressures. For instance, the disgraced army officer, who is handed his sword or revolver, and told to 'do the right thing', has no alternative, whether he wishes to kill himself or not.

Attitudes to suicide have varied greatly throughout history, and in different societies. In ancient Greece, convicted criminals were allowed to take their own lives. In Imperial Rome, suicide was accepted as an honourable death among the aristocracy; but gradually the attitude toward suicide changed, mainly because slaves began to kill themselves, so depriving their masters of what was regarded as valuable property.

Judaic, Christian and Islamic law all declared suicide illegal – in European legal systems it was known as *felo de se* – a crime against the self – but the word 'suicide' (meaning 'killing one-self') was not used in English until 1651. Apart from religious penalties – the denial of burial and other rites – the laws of many countries allowed the official desecration and mutilation of the suicide's body, and the seizing of his or her property. A suicide's body, for example, could not be buried in the hallowed ground of a cemetery, and was sometimes interred at a crossroads – at the boundary between adjoining parishes, so that neither had to take responsibility – with a wooden stake stuck through it, to prevent the unforgiven spirit from wandering.

*FACING PAGE: **Few sights in recent years have provoked more horror than these tumbled corpses found in Jonestown, Guyana, in 1978.** BELOW: **A German general lies dead with a torn picture of Adolf Hitler beside him, after committing suicide as US Army troops entered Leipzig in April 1945.***

The Hindu practice of **suttee**, *in which the widow cast herself voluntarily on to her husband's funeral pyre, was outlawed in India by the British administration in 1829, but it continued, although illegal, until very recent times.*

There were, therefore, a number of reasons – both emotional and financial – why the suicide's relatives should attempt to conceal the cause of death. Suicide, and equally attempted suicide, became a matter for shame and social stigma.

Following the revolution in France in 1789, and the consequent reworking of French laws, attempted suicide was no longer illegal there, and most other European countries gradually followed suit. Nervertheless, it was not until 1961 that the crime of suicide was removed from the statute books in England. For many years before that though, a veil of respectability had been drawn over the illegality by the often used standard coroner's verdict that suicide had been committed 'while the balance of the mind was disturbed'.

In the East, the attitude toward suicide throughout history has been very different. In

THE ATTITUTE TOWARD SUICIDE CHANGED, MAINLY BECAUSE SLAVES BEGAN TO KILL THEM- SELVES, SO DEPRIVING THEIR MASTERS OF VALUABLE PROPERTY

Hinduism, for example, Brahman is the changeless, eternal principle of the cosmos. In the *Upanishads* – the ancient Indian treatises of prose and verse which inquire into the nature of the divine principle and the means of salvation – it is written that, 'The whole universe is Brahman... This my Self within the heart is that Brahman. When I depart from hence I shall merge into it. He who believes this will never doubt.'

The Brahmin sect believe that Brahman is the only true reality, absolutely single and unchanging. Since human lives are rooted in change, they must therefore be unreal and meaningless, and this has always been taken as justification for the toleration of suicide. For centuries *suttee* – the voluntary suicide of an Indian widow on her husband's funeral pyre – was regarded as highly praiseworthy, and was only outlawed in the nineteenth century.

aircraft to crash into Allied warships, became famous during the last months of World War II. One of the most notorious of post-war cases is that of the writer Mishima Yukio (born 1925, real name Hiraoka Kimitake). On 25 November 1970, after delivering the final manuscript of his massive four-part novel *The Sea of Fertility* to his publishers, he and four followers seized control of a military HQ in Tokyo. Mishima made a speech to a thousand soldiers, urging them to overthrow Japan's post war constitution, which forbade war and rearmament. When they did not respond, he then committed voluntary *seppuku* in the traditional way in front of them.

Obligatory *seppuku* was imposed upon samurai found guilty of crime, to spare them the dishonour of being beheaded by the common executioner. It was regularly practised from the fifteenth century until 1873, when it was abolished by law. A witness was required to be present on behalf of the authorities. The prisoner was seated, with a short sword on a table in front of him. Behind him stood a second, usually a relative or friend, with a drawn sword. As soon as the prisoner had stabbed himself – or sometimes as soon as he reached for the sword – the second cut off his head to spare him further pain.

*LEFT: **Mishima Yukio**, with a samurai scarf about his head, delivers his final oration from the balcony of the military HQ in Tokyo, before committing voluntary **seppuku** in November 1970.*

In Japan, *seppuku* ('self-disembowelment') was long considered an honourable end among the samurai, the warrior caste. (It is generally called hara-kiri in the West. The word – which means 'belly cutting' – has the same two ideograms as the word *seppuku*, but in reverse order, and is rarely used by the Japanese.) The correct method of *seppuku* was to thrust a short sword into the left side of the abdomen, then pull it across to the right, and turn it upward. This was followed by a second thrust from below the chest, down to the first cut, and finally a stab into the throat. This relatively slow and agonizing death was regarded as a final demonstration of the courage and unflinching purpose of the samurai.

Voluntary *seppuku* was frequently practised by defeated warriors, to avoid the dishonour of being taken prisoner. Some samurai committed this form of suicide to show their loyalty to commanders who had been killed, as a protest against government policy, or to atone for failure in their duties.

There have been many cases of voluntary *seppuku* in modern Japan. The kamikaze, the 'suicide pilots' who deliberately flew their

*RIGHT: **Hundreds of passers-by watched as a Buddhist monk committed self-immolation, a protest against South Vietnamese government policy, in Saigon in October 1983.***

In recent times, there have also been cases of Buddhist monks and nuns committing suicide by burning themselves alive, as a protest against social and legal conditions in their country. In particular many people remember the horrifying photographs of self-immolation in protest against the war in Vietnam.

Both in the East and in the West, protesting students have also burned themselves alive. The most famous case was the 21-year-old Czech Jan Palach, who publicly set himself alight on 16 January 1969, in protest against the Soviet occupation of his country. More recently, there was a spate of self-immolation at a university in South Korea in the spring of 1991. After two students had set fire to themselves in protest against the beating to death of a fellow student by the police, six more students followed their example until order was restored.

THE CAUSES OF SUICIDE

BELOW: *The Austrian psycho-analyst Sigmund Freud (1856–1939) maintained that it was inner psychological forces, rather than external social forces, that were the cause of suicide.*

Setting aside suicide as a matter of honour or social protest, many modern psychologists and sociologists have attempted to explain the incidence of suicide in the general populace. Emile Durkheim, the French founder of modern sociology, first put forward a set of theories in 1897, which have been expanded by later workers.

Durkheim's theories related to the involvement of the individual with society. He proposed three main types of suicide: egoistic, altruistic, and anomic.

Egoistic suicide is committed by persons who have an inadequate integration with society. They do not accept its rules: they are motivated only by their personal interests, and make their own rules of conduct. Their lives are entirely what they themselves have made them and, if they decide to kill themselves, that is their decision. The disgraced tycoon Robert Maxwell, who committed suicide in November 1990, was clearly of this type.

In contrast, the relatively rare altruistic suicide is the result of over-integration into society, and a corresponding lack of the instinct for self-preservation. The English explorer, Captain Lawrence Oates, fits this type. He was a member of the doomed five-man party commanded by Robert Falcon Scott, which struggled to reach the South Pole in January 1912. On the return journey, the party were snowed-up in their tent; Oates was lamed from severe frostbite, and was concerned that he would delay the others if they were able to move on. With the famous words, 'I am just going outside, and may be some time', he disappeared into the blizzard.

Most common suicides fall into the third, anomic, type. 'Anomie', which comes from the Greek word *anomia* – lawlessness – means a sense

aggression and destruction, he named thanatos. (These two words come respectively from the Greek words for 'love' and 'death'.) Freud suggested that the individual who commits suicide feels aggression and anger over the loss of objects or concepts toward which he or she can no longer extend love. However, instead of expressing this anger externally, the individual turns it inwardly upon himself or herself.

Some behavioural psychologists believe that suicide is a pattern of behaviour, and that it can be learned in the same way as other forms of behaviour. So the tendency to suicide can develop by reinforcement of certain habits and learned associations, accompanied by the lack of reinforcement of more suitable, adaptive behaviour. In this way, suicide can often be adopted by imitation.

The American psychologist Edwin Shneidman investigated similarities between the mental states of suicidal individuals. He identified the existence of thwarted psychological needs, and the feeling that these could not be resolved. He maintained that the suicidal individual failed to see ways of solving the problem, would come to the conclusion that nothing could be done, and so would sink into a condition of hopelessness and helplessness.

At the same time, he believed the sufferer to be ambivalent about suicide, wishing to die but at the same time wanting to continue living. However, there is an unbearable psychological pain – which Shneidman named 'psyache' – from which the individual feels he or she must escape. And the only means of escape is suicide.

One of the strangest aspects of suicide is imitation, which Emile Durkheim was one of the first to observe. He reported how 15 hospital patients had hanged themselves from the same hook in a dark passage of a French regional hospital. When the hook was removed, the number of suicides in the hospital decreased sharply.

of alienation. In normal circumstances, the structure of society provides an individual with a set of conventions to which he or she can conform, and so remain integrated within that society. But circumstances can change. When this happens, the individual may lose all sense of the equilibrium of society, and the social norms that usually guide behaviour. Deprived of such conventions, the individual becomes isolated, and feels that society's rules against suicide no longer apply to him or her, thus giving rise to its possibility.

Durkheim's classification is the sociologist's way of looking at the causes of suicide. Psychologists have different theories.

The Austrian psychoanalyst Sigmund Freud maintained that it was inner psychological forces, rather than external social forces, that caused suicide. He argued that human beings possessed two opposed – but normally balanced – instinctual tendencies. One was the 'life instinct', which he named eros. The other, the tendency toward

FREUD SUGGESTED THAT THE INDIVIDUAL WHO COMMITS SUICIDE FEELS AGGRESSION AND ANGER OVER THE LOSS OF OBJECTS OR CONCEPTS TOWARD WHICH HE OR SHE CAN NO LONGER EXTEND LOVE

ABOVE: *In the month following actress Marilyn Monroe's apparent suicide in August 1962, American authorities reported a 40 per cent increase in suicides in Los Angeles – suspected to have been carried out in imitation.*

RIGHT: *'Kneel, for the Lord approaches' – one of a series of prints to commemorate the journey of the shogun Edo to visit the Japanese emperor in Kyoto in 1863. To remain standing, or even look upon the shogun, could result in instant execution.*

In the month following Marilyn Monroe's death in 1962, American authorities reported a 40 per cent increase in suicides in Los Angeles. In 1978, the Vienna subway saw a number of incidents of suicide; after sensational reports about it in the local press, the rate increased dramatically. The authorities asked the newspapers to tone down their reports on the story. When they did so the suicide rate fell back to its normal level.

But the most extraordinary example of imitation occurred in Japan in the 1930s. When 19-year-old schoolgirl Kiyoko Matsumoto jumped into the crater of a volcano on the island of Oshima, she was soon followed by others, in fact by 143 others. Within two years of the first suicide, the total had reached 1,208 at the same place. Finally, the authorities built a fence around the volcano and it was declared illegal to buy a one-way ticket to the island.

THE INCIDENCE OF SUICIDE

So far as 'normal' suicide is concerned (if any suicide can be described as normal), it seems to have an inescapable relationship with education. For many centuries in Europe, the general populace was virtually deprived of education. They were taught, in church and in the courts of law, to accept their lot and 'know their place' – the rich man in his castle, the poor man at his gate. Whatever they suffered, they were expected –

and, in most cases, agreed – to bear it, as the will of God. Suicide, other than as a matter of honour, was rare; it only otherwise occurred among those who were considered to be extremely psychologically disturbed.

However, as education in Europe and North America became universal, people began to learn to question their circumstances. Some became intensely frustrated by the apparent impossibility of changing things, and by the insensibility of others around them. At the same time, legal and social attitudes toward suicide, and particularly attempted suicide, were changing. When the law (and, perforce, the church) no longer declared suicide to be a crime, it offered itself as a way of demonstrating, publicly, this private frustration.

In the twentieth century, in the more highly developed parts of the world, suicide is seldom regarded as a means of regaining one's honour, or violently demonstrating against official injustice. It is still a form of protest, but in most cases an intensely personal one, a protest against an

LEFT: As a region, Greenland is said to have the highest rate of suicide in the world: 127 per 100,000 people – the bleak, cold climate is believed to contribute to people's depression.

It is for reasons such as these that the incidence of suicide seems to be higher in the more developed countries. Statistics, however, are notoriously unreliable. Figures for any one country depend upon the way in which they are collected. Some coroners may record a verdict of 'accident', rather than suicide, if there is any possibility of doubt. In Catholic countries such as Spain or Ireland, where suicide is still commonly regarded as a sin, relatives and friends, and even the local priest, may conspire to cover up the true circumstances of death.

As a region, Greenland is said to have the highest rate of suicide in the world: 127 per 100,000 people – the climate is supposed to have something to do with it. The relatively high rate in Finland, of 27.8 per 100,000, would seem to support this argument, but rates in Sweden or Norway (popularly supposed to be particularly high) are, at less than 16 per 100,000, no higher than those in Germany (15.5), and lower than those in France (18.9), Switzerland (19.1), and Austria (20.6).

Of the figures published by the World Health Organization, those for Hungary are the highest for any individual country, at 37 per 100,000, but this should be set against the fact that Hungary also comes close to the top of the list for deaths from most kinds of disease, as well as from traffic accidents. The current suicide rate in England and Wales is 7.4 per 100,000 (but 10.8 in Scotland), and 12.3 in the United States.

Even allowing for the possibility that the true cause of death has been covered up,

internal despair from which there appears to be no other escape. And frequently, attempts at suicide are made in the hope that this despair will at last be recognized – perhaps in time for life to be saved.

Another factor has been the increasing availability of the means for taking one's own life. In previous centuries, weapons – such as swords and pistols – were carried only by members of the upper classes, or criminals. Few drugs were available, and – apart from opium and alcohol – were difficult to come by. The commonest means of suicide among the general populace was by drowning – an unattractive, and frequently unsuccessful, method – or hanging. Then, during the nineteenth century, the introduction of coal-gas for lighting and heating quite suddenly introduced a relatively painless method of killing oneself into common society.

Today, anybody who can lay hands on a relatively small amount of money can purchase a handgun. A high percentage of suicides exploit the fact that most doctors, both for their own convenience and that of their patients, are prepared to prescribe large quantities of drugs for use in the patients' own homes. It is sometimes possible that they might be unaware or ignorant of the fact that a patient is of a psychological type that might incline to suicide. With a sufficient amount of a potentially lethal drug at hand, such an individual may well be tempted to end it all.

BELOW: The vast range of drugs that are lethal when taken in excess, but which are made freely available on prescription, is one of the contributory factors in the recent increase in suicide rates.

suicide rates are low in predominantly Roman Catholic countries. Nevertheless, all European countries have shown a steady increase in recent years, including Ireland, Norway and Belgium, and mainly among people under 20 years old. In the United Kingdom, for example, the suicide rates among 15- to 24-year-olds rose by 80 per cent between 1980 and 1992, and four in every five were male. China, on the other hand, has the world's highest rate of female suicides.

Oddly enough, given the eighteenth-century French philosopher Montesquieu's comment that the dismal climate and innate gloominess of the English tied in with the relatively high figures noted there one year, suicide rates today – in Europe, at least – are relatively low in winter, and highest in spring and summer.

MASS SUICIDE

Mass suicide should not be confused with suicide by imitation. At the low end of the scale, a suicide pact between two people demands a high degree of emotional commitment. At a higher level though, involving ten or even a hundred people, there must inevitably be an element of imitation, it is nevertheless ultimately the

outcome of an incredibly intense emotion felt in common with others of a like mind. As mass suicide very often occurs at the same time, it cannot be imitation.

A classic example of mass suicide is found in a story of the Jewish Zealots, who held out against the Romans in the stronghold of Masada in AD 72-73. After being under siege for nearly two years, the 960 men, women and children agreed to die rather than surrender. They drew lots to decide who should die first, and who should be given the responsibility of killing them. Then the executioners drew lots among themselves, until there was just one man left alive. He then stabbed himself, and fell beside his dead family.

There have also been some terrible examples in recent times. James Warren (Jim) Jones established a 'People's Temple' in Indianapolis in 1957. Several years later he moved his followers to California. In 1974, he purchased

BELOW: 'Reverend' Jim Jones, addressing his followers at Jonestown in Guyana, shortly before he ordered them to commit mass suicide.

had formed his sect HIM (Human Individual Metamorphosis) in the 1970s. He relaunched the cult in 1993 with the new name of Heaven's Gate. As the comet Hale-Bopp approached the Earth in March 1997, Applewhite became convinced that a UFO, four times the size of the Earth, was following in its wake. He decided that it was time for his followers to shed their 'earthly containers' and be resurrected on another planet.

Officers from the San Diego Sheriff's Department found 39 bodies, both male and female, at the Heaven's Gate headquarters at Rancho Santa Fe a few miles from San Diego. Their ages ranged from 20 to 72. They had eaten a 'last supper' of chicken pot and cheesecake, followed by a lethal dose of apple juice laced with pentobarbital, washed down with vodka. They they lay down to die with plastic bags over their heads. Beside each of them were overnight bags, containing a change of clothing, a spiral-bound notebook, and a stick of lip-gloss. In each pocket was the sum of $5 – presumably, like the coins given to a corpse in ancient times to pay the ferryman Charon to cross the river Styx, to cover their travel expenses.

*LEFT: **One of the 39 dead bodies being removed from the Rancho Santa Fe headquarters of the Heaven's Gate sect, after their mass suicide in 1997.***

*BELOW: **In Greek myth, the ferryman Charon carried the dead of the underworld across the river Styx, but demanded payment for the ride.***

27,000 acres (11,000 hectares) of rainforest in Guyana, where he founded the colony of Jonestown in 1977. In November 1978, following the murder of five members of an investigation team from the US, Jones ordered his followers to commit 'revolutionary suicide'. They lined up to receive purple Kool-Aid, laced with cyanide, in paper cups. Jones himself was found shot with his family. Reports differ on the number of dead, but it is claimed that, when US Air Force personnel arrived to retrieve the bodies, they found 913 victims.

An equally bizarre mass suicide occurred outside San Diego, California, in April 1997. Former music teacher Marshall H. Applewhite

IN NOVEMBER 1978, JONES ORDERED

HIS FOLLOWERS TO COMMIT

'REVOLUTIONARY SUICIDE'. THEY LINED

UP TO RECEIVE PURPLE KOOL-AID,

LACED WITH CYANIDE,

IN PAPER CUPS

EUTHANASIA

With the increasing acceptance of an individual's right to commit suicide, a pressing problem of medical ethics has arisen. What of someone who, because of physical inability, or lack of suitable means, is unable to take his (or her) life without assistance? In most cases of this kind, the individual is suffering a very painful, and ultimately fatal, disease. Would it not be charitable of the attending physician, or some other person, to provide the means to end the suffering?

One step beyond this lies a question that has already been raised in Chapter 1. When a patient lies in an apparently irreversible coma,

When a patient lies in an apparent irreversible coma, who should decide whether to disconnect the life-support system?

ON GRADUATION, DOCTORS AT

MANY UNIVERSITIES

THROUGHOUT THE WORLD

ARE STILL REQUIRED TO TAKE THE

HIPPOCRATIC OATH. THIS

INCLUDES THE WORDS 'I WILL

GIVE NO DEADLY DRUG TO ANY,

THOUGH IT MAY BE ASKED OF ME'

who is prepared to decide that death is inevitable, and disconnect the support system? And is this a practical and charitable step, or is it something more – is it euthanasia?

The word 'euthanasia' comes from the Greek, meaning 'easy death'. In recent decades it has come to mean deliberately terminating life to avoid unnecessary suffering, and it can be defined as either 'passive' or 'active'. Passive euthanasia is discontinuing the life-sustaining treatment of the sick. Active euthanasia means putting – some might say condemning – to death a person who, due to disease or extreme age, can no longer lead a meaningful life.

On graduation, doctors at many universities throughout the world are still required to take the Hippocratic Oath. This includes the words, 'I will give no deadly drug to any, though it be asked of me, nor will I counsel such… ' Although this is more an ethical code than an 'oath', and contains no threat of punishment, a recognition of its power was contained in the framing, in the past, of many laws that prevented a physician ending the suffering of a patient.

Nowadays, following the lead of Elisabeth Kübler-Ross and others (see Chapter 1), some physicians have become less concerned with prolonging the life of a suffering patient than with providing comfort and relief during the last days. Passive euthanasia for those on the verge of death has gradually become acceptable, following the important recommendations of British and American physicians in 1979 and 1981 (also see Chapter 1).

There were some earlier cases, however. In 1976, the Supreme Court of the American state of New Jersey ruled that, in suitable cases, doctors could disconnect a comatose patient's respirator where it 'prevented the patient from dying with decency and dignity'. The following

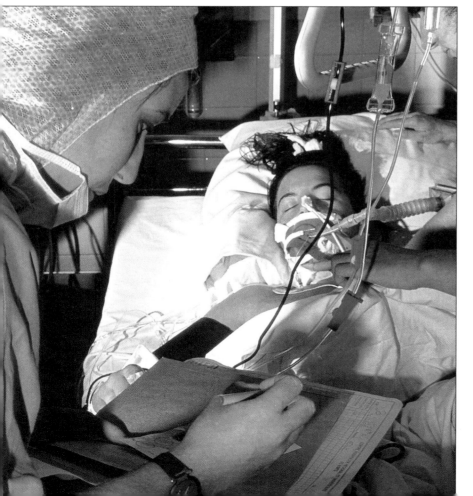

year, 'right to die' bills were introduced by several American state legislatures. More than 30 states have now passed laws, conferring the authority to withdraw life-support upon a family member, friend, legal or religious adviser nominated by the patient, or, in certain cases, upon the decision of the Court.

Finally, in 1990, the US Supreme Court ruled that people who make their wishes known had a constitutional right to have life-support discontinued. Nevertheless, when permanently comatose persons have left no clear instructions, a state may still deny a request by family members to terminate treatment.

In many other countries, there are no laws specifically protecting doctors who practise passive euthanasia, but it is generally agreed that, provided they follow the guidelines of their professional organization, they may discontinue life support. On the other hand, there are few means by which family or friends can legally override the desire of a physician to maintain life.

ACTIVE EUTHANASIA AND 'ASSISTED SUICIDE'

In most countries, with the exception of Uruguay, active euthanasia remains a crime. In the United States, it is punishable by life impris-

LEFT: The form of the Hippocratic Oath adopted by the 3rd General Assembly of the World Medical Association in London in 1949.

onment. In the Netherlands, for over 20 years, the courts did not convict doctors who had helped patients to die at their own request. However, a 1992 survey revealed that, in a single year, more than 1,000 Dutch patients, incapable of giving their consent, had died as a result of their doctor's decision. In 1993 therefore, a new law, while still keeping euthanasia technically illegal, ruled that doctors could not be convicted, provided they notified a coroner of their intentions, and provided the patient was mentally competent, suffering unbearable pain, and had repeatedly requested euthanasia. The doctor also had to consult a second physician before proceeding.

But what of the person who knows that he or she has an incurable disease, and is desperate to avoid the months or years of suffering to come, before the doctors decide to terminate it? Organizations in various countries are agitating for the right of the sufferer to obtain medical assistance in ending it all. One of the best known is the American Hemlock Society (named after the draught of hemlock taken by the Greek philosopher Sophocles), which was founded by Derek Humphry, with the motto 'Death through Dignity', and has over 40,000 members.

In April 1991, Humphry published his book *Final Exit*, a manual of practical advice for those who wished to commit suicide, or wished to help someone else to do so. At first, sales of the

LEFT: Derek Humphry, founder of the American Hemlock Society, and author of the controversial book **Final Exit,** *a manual of practical advice on assisted suicide.*

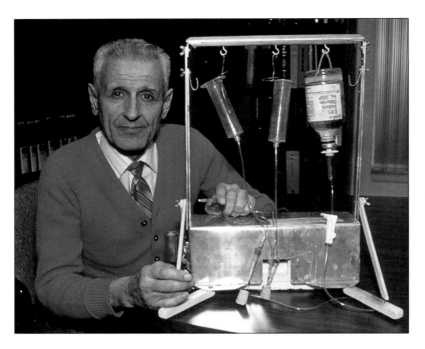

The notorious 'Doctor Death', Jack Kevorkian, demonstrates his home-made device to deliver a lethal injection to a terminal sufferer.

The controversy following the publication of *Final Exit* drew attention to the activities of Dr Jack Kevorkian, who was quickly dubbed 'Doctor Death'. A retired Michigan pathologist, Kevorkian admitted on television that he had helped a sufferer from Alzheimer's disease to commit suicide by connecting her to a home-made device that allowed her to pump lethal potassium chloride into her veins. A Michigan judge decided against prosecuting Kevorkian for murder, but ordered him not to use the device again. 'Doctor Death' got round the ruling by using an alternative method, this time a mask attached to a cylinder of carbon monoxide, and continued his one-man crusade for assisted suicide.

However, the publicity Kevorkian provoked, together with his obviously slapdash methods, had the effect of turning public opinion against the concept. Several states already had draft legislation for medically assisted suicide which, in the wake of the controversy, was quickly thrown out. In Michigan a hurriedly-passed law made assisted suicide punishable by up to four years in prison, and a $2000 fine. It was clearly directed at Kevorkian. He reacted to this by claiming that he remained alone with his patient during the 'operation', and then left the scene discreetly and make an anonymous telephone call to alert the emergency services to the death.

book were low, but following an article in the *Wall Street Journal* and television reports, the first edition of 41,000 copies sold out, and by August the book topped the bestseller list of 'how-to' books in the *New York Times*.

Humphry urged doctors and nurses that it was right to assist the 'self-deliverance' of terminally ill patients. He argued, 'Part of good medicine is to help you out of this life, as well as help you in. When cure is no longer possible and the patient seeks relief through euthanasia, the help of physicians is most appropriate.'

Accused of encouraging suicide among the emotionally unstable, Humphry denied the accusation. He said, 'My book pleads with the depressed to go to a psychiatrist. But it's addressed to the 6,000 who die every day, not the handful who commit suicide.' He insisted that his book did not make suicide easier – but more reliable, less painful, and above all, less solitary. He asked those who decided to elect for suicide to gather family and friends around them, for final solace.

IN 1998, KEVORKIAN PERSUADED AN AMERICAN TV NETWORK NEWS PROGRAMME TO SHOW A FILM OF HIM ADMINISTERING A FATAL INJECTION TO A TERMINALLY ILL CANCER PATIENT

In 1998, Kevorkian persuaded an American TV network news programme to show a film of him administering a fatal injection to a terminally ill cancer patient. Responding to criticism of the film from advertisers and church leaders, Kevorkian said, 'This could never be a crime in a society that deems itself enlightened'. He was subsequently arrested and received two years' probation and a $900 fine, the punishment being for 'misdemeanor, assault and resisting arrest' rather than anything more serious. He pledged to continue his crusade for legalizing assisted suicide, and in March 1999 he was finally found guilty of murder.

Meanwhile, a 1993 report in the *New England Journal of Medicine* had raised some disturbing questions about *Final Exit*. One of the methods recommended in the book was self-asphyxiation in a plastic bag. A study by Cornell Medical Center found that, in the year following the book's publication, suicides committed in this way rose by 30 per cent across the United States. Out of 144 cases of suicide in New York City, at least 15 of the victims were known to have consulted the book, and of these six had no recorded medical problems. On the other hand, proponents of euthanasia point out that the suicide rate as a whole remained unchanged.

In 1994, a landmark case occurred in the Netherlands. Following the passing of the 1993 law, it was calculated that there were some 2,300 cases of euthanasia and 400 cases of assisted suicide each year. But in almost all of these cases, patients were suffering from a terminal illness or unbearable physical pain. Then psychiatrist Boudewijn Chabot admitted that he had helped a healthy woman to die because she suffered from depression.

Hilly Bosscher was 50 years old, and had already made an unsuccessful attempt to kill herself. She was adamant that all she wanted was to die. Chabot spent four months attempting to relieve her depression, but she did not respond, and refused to take drugs – unless Chabot would prescribe something with which she could end her life. At last he agreed. Hilly Bosscher took her leave of this world lying on her bed, with Chabot and another doctor sitting beside her. To the sound of the music of Bach, she kissed a photograph of her two dead sons, and then gently slipped into death.

Although Chabot had violated all the guidelines of the 1993 law – he had not, for example,

Australian doctor Phillip Nitschke, with the computer-controlled apparatus used by 22-year-old Bob Dent to commit suicide in 1996.

consulted a second physician – the Dutch high court ruled that he was not to be punished. As Chabot pointed out: 'intolerable psychological suffering is no different from intolerable physical suffering.'

In the Northern Territory of Australia, Dr Phillip Nitschke has been a pioneer in assisted euthanasia. An Act entitled 'Right of the Terminally Ill' was passed in the state in 1996. The first person to take advantage of it was 22-year-old Bob Dent, who suffered from cancer of the prostate. He was able to take his life by clicking commands onto a computer that activated a machine to administer lethal drugs intravenously. Three others were able to exploit the Act, before it was overturned by the Federal Parliament in 1997, on the grounds that it could be open to abuse, particularly in terms of the rights of the indigenous Aboriginal population, for whom euthanasia is at best murder and at worst sorcery. Now Dr Nitschke is reported to have built a 'coma machine' that will automatically deliver drugs to patients, keeping them comatose until they die.

Also in 1997, the British Medical Association (BMA) requested police to investigate the activities of two well-respected English doctors. The doctors had announced that, after discussing matters with relatives, they had both given patients lethal doses of painkilling drugs – relieving their suffering and hastening their deaths. One had provided his patients with a 'customized exit bag', containing a lethal dose of the drug Temazepam.

A member of the BMA Medical Ethics Committee pronounced that this 'amounted to execution'. However, any prosecution for murder would have to establish that a doctor planned to kill his patient, and this would be difficult in cases where a commonly prescribed painkiller was used as the agent of death.

DID HE FALL, OR WAS HE PUSHED?

When a person is found dead, the cause of death must be determined by autopsy. The word 'autopsy' means 'seeing for oneself', and this is exactly what the pathologist at the mortuary must do. It is not enough to guess at the cause of death, or to assume that the appearance of the body, or the conditions in which it was found, make the cause obvious. A full examination of the bone structure, the tissues and the internal organs, has to be undertaken in order to discover whether death was the result of something other than the apparent cause.

Most particularly, the pathologist has to determine whether death was the result of disease, suicide – or even murder. There are many recorded cases in which a murderer has attempted to disguise his work as suicide. For instance, a body found in a river, a lake or the sea – presumed drowned – may have been already dead or unconscious when it was consigned to the water. Death by shooting, even when the weapon is found clutched in the victim's hand, must always be investigated carefully.

Conversely, there are cases where the circumstances would seem to indicate murder, but which are found to be suicide (see page 20). Self-strangulation with a thin cord is not uncommon. And someone may even plan his or her suicide to look like murder, so that relations can still benefit from a life insurance.

The eminent Scottish pathologist Sir Sydney Smith described a number of bizarre cases of suicide that he had encountered during his long working life:

Cutting through the tissues at the back of the neck with a blunt knife might be thought a rather absurd way of attempting to kill oneself, but I saw a case once… In another odd case a maid in a hospital hacked the front of her head, inflicting 20 cuts; then, finding this ineffective, she filled a bath with warm water and drowned herself. I wonder how many of us doctors, finding a number of hatchet wounds in the skull, would think of suicide.

Smith also wrote of a case in which a man was found dead from hanging. He had a bullet wound on the side of his face, and another in the palm of one hand; five cuts in his throat, and cuts in his wrist. Nevertheless, it became clear from the circumstances that he had committed suicide. After attempting to shoot himself with a pistol, and then cut his throat and wrists, he had finally, in desperation, hanged himself.

In his lectures to medical students, Smith would often conclude with a case, not one of his own, but learned from one of his colleagues, in which a man decided to hang himself from the branch of a tree stretching out over the sea. First he took a large dose of opium to dull the pain, and then decided to make certain by shooting himself as well.

The noose adjusted, the poison taken, and the revolver cocked, he stepped over the cliff, and as he did so he fired. The jerk of the rope altered his aim, and the bullet missed his head and cut partly through the rope. This broke with the jerk of the body, and he fell 50 feet into the sea below. There he swallowed a quantity of salt water, vomited up the poison, and swam ashore – a better and a wiser man.

THE AUTOPSY

The thorough dissection of a dead body that a pathologist has to undertake is frequently the cause of great distress to relatives, but it must be done. (For obvious reasons, the body is usually released in a closed coffin after autopsy, although modern embalming techniques can subsequently make it possible for relatives to view the corpse.)

First of all comes the external examination. The pathologist will carefully record the appearance of the body, noting any marks, bruises or wounds, as well as the position of hypostasis (see page 18), and the condition of the eyes. In cases of suicide or suspected murder, swabbed specimens will be taken from such sites as the hands, mouth, breasts, vagina and rectum. These will subsequently be analyzed. Nowadays, all the pathologist's observations and comments made during the course of an autopsy are recorded on tape.

The autopsy room of a modern American mortuary is provided with all the necessary equipment for a rapid post mortem examination.

The first stage of the internal examination is to make a large Y-shaped incision, which begins behind each ear and extends down the sternum as far as the groin. This enables the pathologist to peel the skin back easily, exposing the neck and chest, and revealing the bones, muscles and organs inside the body. It will also expose any subcutaneous bruising that may not have been apparent during the initial external examination.

In order to remove the lungs, heart and other organs for subsequent examination and analysis, the breastbone must be cut through. After this, the skull must be opened. The initial incision is continued across the top of the head, and the skin of the scalp pulled away to expose the bone. A circular saw is used to cut round the skull, and the top is prized off. The pathologist examines the brain and the inside of the skull minutely for evidence of injury – traces of old injuries can sometimes give a clue to the victim's previous lifestyle. The brain is then removed for further examination.

When the autopsy has been completed, the body is reconstructed as closely as possible to its original state. Sterile packing is inserted in place of the removed organs, and the body is tightly stitched together before delivery to the undertaker – although if the cause of death is not quickly determined a coroner's inquest may require the body to be kept many months preserved in the mortuary. The purpose of the reconstruction of the body is to make it acceptable for the funeral process – in some cases, such as fatal car crashes and other disasters, the appearance of the body may be improved by this reconstruction.

The whole autopsy process, apart from the reconstruction, can normally be completed in half an hour (though the twentieth-century English pathologist Francis Camps claimed that he could do it in ten minutes). The subsequent examination, usually by other members of the pathology team, including toxicologists, will, of course, take much longer. A hospital autopsy will usually only confirm the apparent cause of death, but one carried out under police instructions is particularly concerned to establish whether the victim died by his or her own hand, or by violence.

SPONTANEOUS COMBUSTION

One of the strangest forms of unnatural death, indeed one whose occurrence is denied by many scientists, despite considerable evidence, is spontaneous combustion. Usually, the victims are found burned to death, with much of the body reduced to ashes, but with their surroundings scarcely touched by fire. Given these extraordinary circumstances it is particularly interesting to read an objective account

of his leg. He slapped at it fiercely without success, then closed his hands over it to starve it of oxygen. Eventually the flame was extinguished, to Hamilton's immense relief.

The phenomenon is relatively rare, but examples have been reported over several centuries, despite continuing scepticism from fire officers and doctors. Generally, the victims have been elderly, found indoors, with most or all of the body no more than a pile of ash. Carpet and floorboards beneath the body are burnt through, and if they have been sitting in a chair, then that too will have been consumed in the fire. But the rest of the room, even inflammable materials close by, will be untouched, although probably stained with soot.

> SPONTANEOUS COMBUSTION IS RELATIVELY RARE, BUT EXAMPLES HAVE BEEN REPORTED OVER SEVERAL CENTURIES, DESPITE CONTINUING SCEPTICISM FROM FIRE OFFICERS AND DOCTORS

During the night of 1 July 1951, Mrs Mary Reeser, a 67-year-old widow from St Petersburg in Florida, burnt to death in her armchair. The chair had burnt down to its springs, and there was nothing left of Mrs Reeser but a pile of ashes. A small circle of carpet was charred, and there was a circle of soot on the ceiling. A pile of papers found nearby was not even scorched.

Dr Wilton M. Krogman, a forensic expert, commented:

> *I cannot conceive of such complete cremation without more burning of the apartment itself. In fact, the apartment and everything in it should have been consumed ... I regard it as the most amazing thing I have ever seen. As I review it, the short hairs on my neck bristle with faint fear. Were I living in the Middle Ages, I'd mutter something about black magic.*

The sparse remains of Dr J. Irving Bentley, a 93-year-old physician of Coudersport, Pennsylvania, were found in his bathroom on the morning of 5 December, 1966. A hole a little less than a metre across had burnt right through the floor to the basement below. The deputy coroner reported, 'All I found was a knee joint

written by someone who actually survived the phenomenon.

One cold morning in January 1835, James Hamilton, professor of mathematics at the University of Nashville in the United States, was reading the meteorological instruments on the porch of his house. Suddenly, he felt 'a steady pain like a hornet sting, accompanied by a sensation of heat' in his left leg. He looked down and saw a bright blue flame 'about the size of a dime in diameter' springing several inches out

All that remained of Dr J. Irving Bentley on the morning of 5 December, 1966: one leg, still in its slipper, and his walking frame. The very small burnt area of floor is characteristic of such cases of 'spontaneous combustion'.

An illustration by Phiz in Charles Dickens's **Bleak House.** *The last traces of rag-and-bone dealer Krook, totally consumed by spontaneous combustion, are discovered in his sordid room.*

broken log of wood sprinkled with white ashes, or is it coal? Oh Horror he is here! and this from which we run away, striking out the light and overturning one another into the street, is all that represents him.

The celebrated German chemist Justus von Liebig investigated the strange phenomenon, although he refused to believe in it, on the grounds that he had never personally observed it. Nevertheless, he proved by experiment that alcohol-saturated flesh will burn only until the alcohol is consumed.

Other explanations came from the medical profession. The most favoured is that the fire is fuelled by the body's fatty tissues; and a report suggested that the reason the upper body is often consumed, leaving the legs, or some part of the legs untouched, is 'a "candle effect", in which fat from the ignited head of the body saturates clothing, which acts as a wick'.

An alternative suggestion from the medical profession is found in a report in the journal *Applied Trophology*, published in December 1957. This proposes that spontaneous combustion is due to the build-up of phosphagens – compounds of amino acids with phosphoric acid that are involved in the complex biochemical reactions of muscle contraction. 'Phosphagen is a compound like nitroglycerine … It is no doubt so highly developed in certain sedentary persons as to make their bodies actually combustible, subject to ignition, burning like wet gunpowder under some circumstances.'

There is, however, an important drawback to this explanation, and that is that phosphagens are completely unrelated to nitroglycerine.

Many alleged cases of spontaneous combustion are found, on closer investigation, to be attributable to contact with a naked flame. However, there is a sufficient number of incidents where this is clearly not the case, where no one knows how the fire originated, there is no explanation for the intensity of the heat, which needs to be equal to that produced in a crematorium furnace, and yet leaves the surroundings untouched.

atop a post in the basement, the lower leg from the knee down, and the now-scattered ashes 6 feet below.' Yet Dr Bentley's walking frame was standing untouched beside the hole, and the bathtub, only about a foot away, was only slightly scorched.

During the nineteenth century, it was believed that heavy drinking produced a concentration of inflammable substances in the body's tissues; and this was certainly the reason given by Charles Dickens for the combustion of his character Krook in a celebrated incident in the novel *Bleak House*:

> There is very little fire left in the grate, but there is a smouldering suffocating vapour in the room and a dark greasy coating on the walls and ceiling. The chairs and table, and the bottle so rarely absent from the table, all stand as usual … Here is a small burnt patch of flooring; here is the tinder from a little bundle of burnt paper … and here is – is it the cinder of a small charred and

SACRIFICE

Thankfully one form of violent death, human sacrifice, is nowadays virtually unknown, even in the most remote parts of the globe. At one time or another, however, it has been a part of the history of nearly every form of religion.

The word 'sacrifice' comes from the Latin; it denotes an object or living creature that has been made holy (*sacer*) by its dedication to a god or gods. A sacrifice can be offered as a gift, as an act of atonement, or to establish a form of communion. In practice, more than one of these aspects is involved at the same time; the giving of a gift is in itself an attempt to establish communion, an act of atonement requires the giving up of something that one values.

To ensure a good crop, sacrificial victims were buried in the fields; to protect a new building, they were entombed in its foundations. In nineteenth-century Africa, an Ashanti king was reported to have killed 200 young girls and mixed their blood in the mortar of his palace walls to make it impregnable. In ancient Japan, victims were known as 'human pillars'. The Vikings, and several Polynesian peoples, were said to launch their new boats over the bound bodies of their captives.

The concept of ensuring the fertility of crops was also extended to human fertility. In some cultures, the first-born male child was sacrificed to ensure that his mother bore additional sons. At one time in India, the children of low-caste persons might be sacrificed so that the wife of an eminent man would conceive.

Making a gift to the gods, to ensure their benevolence, was another reason for human sacrifice. The Old Testament describes how children were burnt by the Canaanites as offerings to Baal. The ancient Greeks had a special class of victims, the *pharmakoi*, who were kept in readiness for sacrifices to avert disasters such as plague or famine. And Adam of Brehmen, writing in the eleventh century, described how 'it is customary to solemnise at Uppsala, at nine-year intervals, a general feast of all the provinces of Sweden…The sacrifice is of this nature: of every living thing that is male, they offer nine heads, with the blood of which it is customary to placate gods of this sort. The bodies they hang in the sacred grove that adjoins the temple. Even dogs and horses hang there with men.'

*ABOVE: **In the Aztec ritual of sacrifice to the sun, the victims' hearts were cut out by a priest, and their blood flowed in a river down the steps of the Great Pyramid in Tenochititlán.***
*LEFT: **According to Roman authors, the ancient Druids carried out human sacrifice. Here, in a historical pageant held in England in 1932, an actor re-enacts the imagined scene.***

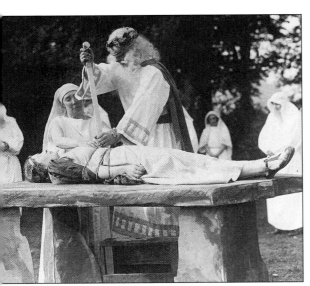

55

In Central America, the painted walls of pre-Columbian Mayan temples show scenes of religious sacrifices, usually of plants or animals, but some depict human sacrifice, the victim's heart being torn out, and its blood allowed to flow. Worshippers would also offer their own blood, but in smaller amounts, usually taken from their ears or tongue.

The religion of the Aztecs was similar to that of the Maya, but human sacrifice appears to have been the most important part of it. Blood was the source of the sun's energy. He had to be fed, cooled and kept in motion by the 'red cactus-fruit' – human hearts and blood. If sacrifices were not made regularly the sun would stay still in the sky, and the human race would perish from his fire.

Although it was considered a great honour to be sacrificed to the sun, many of the victims in the major ceremonies were enemy warriors, captured in battle and brought back to the Great Pyramid in Tenochtitlán. One by one, they were led up the steps of the pyramid, through clouds of incense. One by one, their hearts were ripped out with an obsidian knife, and a river of blood flowed down the steps. Their heads were cut off, and ranged in great skull racks.

A different aspect of sacrifice was the custom of expecting retainers to join their master in the tomb, in order to serve him in the afterlife. A Scythian king was buried with his entire household. In the royal cemetery of the Sumerian city of Ur, 16 graves were excavated, containing from six to 70 victims. Two tombs of Chinese kings have been found to contain more than 100 bodies each, and this practice continued until the thirteenth century. At the funeral of Attila the Hun, in AD 453, 500 mounted warriors are said to have cut their throats in order to follow him.

How voluntarily human beings offered themselves for sacrifice remains an open question. The self-sacrifice of Attila's warriors is very similar to the *seppuku* of the Japanese samurai (see page 39), and no doubt it was expected of them – social pressures, the emotion of a great public occasion, the example of others, all these were contributory factors. But as the solitary victim gradually prepared for a ritual death, how did he feel?

EXECUTION

No matter whether it approaches slowly or quickly, the moment of death comes suddenly for us all. But no death is more sudden than decapitation by the guillotine, and there are some strange stories concerning the victims of this method of execution.

During the nineteenth century, several French professors and medical men suggested that the blade of the guillotine cut through the neck so swiftly that, possibly, the 'life force' continued to flow for some time in the brain.

As Geoffrey Abbott has written in *The Book of Execution* (1994):

Perhaps a victim actually saw the basket coming up to meet him; was aware of the triumphant shouts of the crowd; maybe even heard the gushing sound of his own blood pumping from his gaping neck and splashing on to the boards of the scaffold. And, because the severed vocal chords prevented him from speaking, perhaps, if one were to

conduct experiments at the very moment of decapitation, maybe the victim could indicate in some manner that his brain still functioned.

A gruesome experiment along these lines was carried out in 1907 by a certain Dr Amirault. He circulated blood from a living dog into the head of an executed criminal named Menesclou. He reported that 'the lips filled out, the eyelids twitched, and after two hours the dog's blood had reactivated a living brain, and speech was possibile, for the lips contracted, as if about to speak.'

When the murderer Magret was guillotined, his head fell conveniently upright in the basket. The attending doctor, Marcoux, described how he observed the eyelids and lips still twitching. He put his mouth

'THE EXECUTIONER PLUCKED OUT HIS HEART AND ACCORDING TO THE MANNER HELD IT UP SAYING, "HERE IS THE HEART OF A TRAITOR", SIR EVERARD MADE ANSWER, "THOU LIEST"'

close to one ear, and called Magret's name clearly. At this, the eyes opened, and, 'he looked at me, focusing for 10 to 15 seconds – not a glassy stare, but one of deliberate attention. Then the eyelids closed, but, when his name was called again, the eyes opened once more, following me as I moved around the basket. And then the eyes closed again, never to reopen.'

Modern medical opinion is that these varied anecdotes merely describe the involuntary twitching of the muscles after death – after all, it is a part of folklore that chickens, swiftly decapitated with a knife, will continue to run about the farmyard for some seconds afterward. As Dr Harold Hillman, of the University of Surrey, has pointed out:

The eyes of small rodents move for a few seconds after biochemists have guillotined them. Anaesthetised sheep lose the flash-evoked responses of their electrocorticographs about 14 seconds after both carotid arteries are severed, and 70 seconds after one carotid artery and one jugular vein are cut. Dogs become unconscious 12 seconds after the blood supply to their brains is occluded. It has been calculated that the human brain has enough oxygen stored for metabolism to persist about seven seconds after the supply is cut off. However, the brain could well derive some of its energy from substrate in the scalp and facial and neck muscles.

Finally, here is a somewhat different story. When Sir Everard Digby was hanged for his part in the Gunpowder Plot – the 1605 attempt on the life of King James I of England and VI of Scotland – he was said to be still conscious when he was cut down to be drawn and quartered. According to a later description by seventeenth-century antiquarian Anthony à Wood, 'When the executioner plucked out his heart and according to the manner held it up saying, "Here is the heart of a traitor", Sir Everard made answer, "Thou liest".'

The scene at Versailles, France, in August 1922. The serial killer Henri Landru ('the French Bluebeard') is led to his execution by guillotine before a crowd of officials.

CHAPTER 4

THE RITUALS OF DEATH

In any society the ritual surrounding death is one of a number of social events that anthropologists define as 'rites of passage'. In his seminal work *Les Rites de Passage* (1909), French ethnographer and folklorist Arnold Van Gennep described how each rite could be divided into three phases. The significance of his analysis was that – no matter how the finer details may differ in various communities around the world – the generalities of behaviour around the time of someone's death remain the same.

The first phase is death itself, in which both the deceased and the mourners become separated from their previous social condition. The second Van Gennep described as a 'marginal' phase, during which mourners adopt special modes of behaviour and dress, while the spirit of the dead person is believed to be either making a long journey, or lingering, rootless and restless, close to home. In the third phase, the mourners return to their previous social state, while the spirit of the departed is supposed to have reached its ultimate destination: which can then be marked by a further form of ritual.

However, although Van Gennep's model serves well as a description of the events that take place after death, there are two very different interpretations of the motivation for these events.

The anthropologist Bronislaw Malinowski proposed that funeral customs were a social mechanism allowing a relief of emotional tension – a simple readjustment of normal conditions. Death provokes strong and conflicting emotions: on the one hand a horror of death but on the other a persisting love for the departed; a desire to sever ties with the dead, but also to maintain them. These find expression in the funeral rites, 'which endorse and duplicate the natural feelings of the survivors: they create a social event out of a natural fact'. Malinowski suggested that the rituals – and their related religious significance – were intended to counteract 'the centrifugal forces of fear, dismay and demoralization', and were 'the most powerful means of reintegration of the group's shaken solidarity, and of the re-establishment of its morale'.

A virtually opposite view is taken by sociologists, following the lead of Emile Durkheim. He pointed out that socially dictated expressions of grief were often out of all proportion to the strength of individual emotions: they tended, not to relieve, but to enhance the tension. Durkheim maintained that the purpose of ritual was not to release emotions, but to

FACING PAGE:
In different communities, death is marked by a wide variety of rituals. Here, at the Dilgo Kyentse Gompa in Kathmandu, Nepal, the death of the Tibetan lama Urgen Tulku in 1996 is marked with a solemn dance.

BELOW: The surviving relics of someone long dead retain some part of their personality. This Bulgarian reliquary is believed to enclose part of the skull of St John the Baptist.

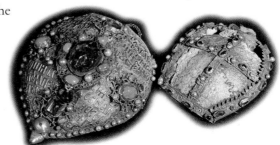

ABOVE: *Public expression of intense grief is an important part of the ritual of death in many communities.*

create them and express them, in this way affirming the fundamental values of society. For example, the public grief of a widow – which may take the form of unrelieved wailing, self-laceration, or even shared death on her husband's funeral pyre – serves to reassert the importance of the conjugal ties.

Many modern psychologists hold a position midway between these two theories. They suggest that many funeral customs reflect a subconscious awareness of guilt and fear – and, above all, the need to get rid of the feeling that the death was, in some way, half desired.

Whatever the explanation, there is little doubt that there is an ambivalence in funeral customs: on the one hand, they expose an instinctive horror of death, and even of the dead; on the other, they reveal a desire to maintain some kind of bond with the departed. Although

the corpse is known to be a source of pollution, the mourners may touch it, kiss it, even anoint themselves with its fluids. At the same time, the funeral rites – prayers, offerings of food, and other rituals – are designed to speed the deceased on the way to his or her final destination, and so finally be rid of him or her, and prevent any possibility of an unwelcome return.

In some cultures, domestic utensils are buried with the corpse, and any other property belonging to them is destroyed. In a practical sense, this avoids the problems of inheritance; but it also helps to establish the final separation of the dead from the world of the living.

In spite of this need to be rid of the dead, there remains a desire to amongst the living to re-establish some kind of relationship – a relationship that is often justified in the belief that the spirit of the deceased can protect and assist the survivors. Among ancient or more primitive cultures, this relationship might be maintained in a purely physical way. The body could be preserved whole as a mummy (and, even in recent centuries in Europe, the absence of decay within the tomb was persuasive evidence for the canonization of a saint by the Catholic Church), the skull might be kept in a place of honour, or bones, hair or pieces of skin worn as amulets.

RIGHT: *In dry conditions, a dead body may mummify without decay. Many wealthy citizens and churchmen – some 8,000 in all – were interred in the catacombs of Palermo, Sicily.*

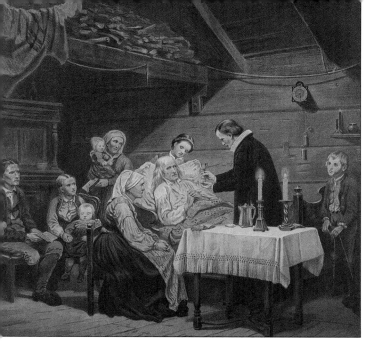

Other ways of maintaining a relationship with the dead can be wholly spiritual. The belief in a protective guardian spirit is the basis of ancestor worship in Chinese and other cultures (see page 115). Some aspects of Spiritualism (see page 118) also reflect this belief. Even in the modern, intensely materialistic, world this instinct survives as a desire to see, and perhaps touch, any surviving relic of someone, long dead, whose achievements are regarded as inspiring veneration. One outstanding example of this is the thousands of people who crowd each year into the house in Salzburg where Mozart was born, to view the musical scores and instruments that were – perhaps – touched by the hand of the great composer.

AT THE HOUR OF DEATH

When death comes naturally it seldom comes unexpectedly. Relatives, the doctor, the priest, often even the dying person – all are aware that death is imminent. In all parts of the world, there are specific rites that must be performed at this time. Their purpose is to ease the last moments of the dying man or woman, to reassure them that they are, and will continue to be, loved, to relieve their conscience of guilt, and to promise them that their spirit will find peace.

Once death has occurred, there are other rites to be performed. In many parts of Europe, for example, it is still customary to stop all the clocks in the house; extinguish the fire in the hearth; and close blinds or curtains to cover the windows – and, sometimes, even the mirrors. (The motivation for these practices may be a surviving atavistic intention to avoid confusing the spirit of the departed, which is considered to linger close to the dead body.)

Religious or civil law often defines the time that must elapse between the moment of death and the disposal of the body. During this time, the corpse may be washed, dressed in its best clothing, wrapped in a shroud, and left lying in state. Frequently, lights and ritual objects are placed around it. Different social customs will require expressions of intense grief, or religious ceremonies, even a feast – the Irish wake is a surviving contemporary example of this, to celebrate the passing of a life.

DISPOSAL OF THE BODY

Even within a single culture, there may be more than one method laid down for the disposal of a dead body. The ceremonies attending the disposal, and the means of disposal itself, can depend not only on the person's position in society, but also on the circumstances of death. An extreme instance of this can be found among the Nuer of the Sudan, who normally practise burial, but where stillborn twins will rather be

*LEFT: **When death comes naturally, relatives, the doctor, the priest and often even the dying person are all aware that it is imminent. There are rites to be performed at this time that will ease the passage for both the dying and the living.***

*BELOW: **In some parts of the world coffins do not always take a simple familiar form. When he died in Chicago in 1984, the body of Willie 'Wimp' Stokes was seated upright at the wheel of a coffin fashioned to resemble a Cadillac.***

placed in the fork of a tree. Some peoples classify the aged, or those who have been ill for a long time, as being 'dead' already; and these unfortunate individuals may even be buried while still alive.

Perhaps the oldest method of disposing of a dead body is by burial in the ground. Naturally, burial is just about the only evidence we have of the funeral practices of the earliest prehistoric peoples, but the evidence accords with what has been observed in surviving primitive cultures. The body may be laid in a sleeping position, or it may be bent – or even tied – into a foetal position, possibly implying the idea of a subsequent rebirth. Sometimes it is sitting, or even standing upright. It is often sprinkled or surrounded with red ochre, which may also symbolize the life force.

The belief in some kind of life after death is also evidenced by way in which food, ornaments, domestic utensils, weapons – even the bodies of servants – are buried with the corpse. The use of a cave, or a specially constructed tomb of large stones or rocks, as the place of burial suggests that this is regarded as a 'house' for the departed.

Cremation is the common means of disposal among Hindus, and is also practised by many Buddhists. In ancient Egypt and China, Israel and Islam, cremation was, and is, forbidden for various reasons: the need to ensure immortality by the preservation of the body, the requirements of the cult of ancestor worship, or a belief in the possibility of physical resurrection.

In prehistoric Europe, cremation gradually replaced burial toward the end of the Bronze Age – cemeteries dating from this time have been discovered with hundreds of urns containing ashes – and this trend continued in Greek and Roman times. The method was abandoned with the rise of Christianity, which adopted many Judaic practices, but has returned to favour since the nineteenth century (see page 71).

ABOVE: The ancient Egyptians raised the techniques of mummification to a fine art, removing the organs and embalming the remains.

*ABOVE: **Cremation is the means of disposal of the dead body practised by Hindus. Ideally, it should be carried out on the banks of the sacred river Ganges.***

In ancient Egypt, bodies were originally buried, clothed and provided with food and domestic utensils. It was the discovery that the hot, dry sand was capable of preserving the intact body that led to the practice of mummification. As Egyptian funeral ceremonies became more elaborate, stone tombs (*mastabas*) were erected for the most important personages. But the atmosphere inside these tombs could not protect the body from corruption, and artificial techniques of preservation had to be developed.

It was not only in Egypt that mummification was practised. The Incas of South America tightly tied and wrapped bodies after drying them, to protect them from the destructive influence of the earth in which they were buried. In many parts of the world, this practice was reserved for high-ranking personages, such as kings and priests. Even among the Australian Aborigines of Torres Strait, mummification was practised until recent times.

Embalming is similar to mummification. The embalmed bodies of Lenin and (for a time) Stalin on show in the Moscow Kremlin became famous objects of pilgrimage for many thousands of Russians, as well as visitors from other countries.

What must seem, to many people, to be an uncaring means of disposal is to expose a body to the open air, but the cultures that adopted this method had sound religious reasons for doing so. The Mandans of North America laid their dead on open scaffolds, built just high enough to be out of the reach of scavenging animals (but accessible to buzzards and other carrion-eating birds). When the bones were clean, the skull was placed with others in a circle, where friends and relatives could bring offerings to honour their dead.

Similar methods, using a platform for corpses, are still used in other parts of the world. Orthodox Parsees, Indian practitioners of Zoroastrianism, believe that neither earth, fire nor water should be defiled by corpses. They place their dead on 'towers of silence', where they are exposed to the sun and to the circling vultures.

Committing a dead body to water continues to be the usual Western practice for those who die aboard ship. This habit grew from the impracticality of preserving a body during a long voyage, but inevitably it had superstitious overtones. Sailors believed that a corpse aboard attracted bad weather or, at very least, contrary winds. When one sea captain had to transport the body of the Bishop of Derry, he hid the fact from his crew by having the coffin put into a crate labelled 'antique statue'.

Burial at sea was the fate of Francis Drake, 'slung betweeen the roundshot in Nombre Dios Bay'. Horatio Nelson's corpse, on the other hand, was sealed in a cask of brandy, after his death at Trafalgar in 1805, and shipped back to England for a hero's funeral.

A very different reason for sea burial was advanced by a New Englander, Samuel Baldwin. On 20 May 1736, in response to his earnest request, his body was consigned to the waves off the New Hampshire coast, expressly to disappoint the wishes of his wife. In the course of frequent domestic arguments, she had told him that, if she survived him, she would take the greatest pleasure in dancing on his grave.

In some parts of the world, throwing a body into water is a way of getting rid of the corpses of people of little account: lepers, slaves, foreigners or criminals. Among the Pacific islands, there are coastal stretches set aside as cemeteries; corpses may be wrapped for protection, and weighted with stones. In the Solomons, however, they are placed on the reef, to be consumed by sharks.

Another way of committing a body to water was to launch it aboard a raft or canoe. This became symbolized in the building of boat-shaped tombs or coffins, or the use of an actual ship for burial on land. In this way – practised

HORATIO NELSON'S CORPSE WAS SEALED IN A CASK OF BRANDY AFTER HIS DEATH AT TRAFALGAR IN 1805, AND SHIPPED BACK TO ENGLAND FOR A HERO'S FUNERAL

Like the former Mandans of North America, and present-day Parsees, Tibetans expose their dead in a 'sky burial', leaving the remains to be consumed by vultures.

ABOVE: In many cultures, the dead are carried to the grave in the simplest possible way, without ritual garments or a coffin, as in this funeral in Papua New Guinea.

in general by seafaring peoples such as the Vikings – the deceased was sent on his last voyage to the afterlife.

One final means of disposing of the dead body must be mentioned, and that is cannibalism. In certain parts of the Pacific region, it was seen as a way of ensuring that the dead person remained in close union with his people, and it remained an obligation on his surviving relatives. The body was consumed at a funeral feast. Of the inhabitants of eastern New Guinea it was once said, 'their cemeteries are their bellies'. (Some faint echo of this practice may perhaps be found in the old Welsh custom of paying a 'sin eater' to eat bread and cheese, or a cake, and drink a mug of ale over the coffin, thus symbolically consuming the sins of the dead.)

FUNERAL CEREMONIES

ANCIENT EGYPT

When a rich Egyptian or a member of his family died, the body was embalmed and mummified. The internal organs – liver, lungs, stomach and intestines, but not the heart, which was left in place – were removed through an incision in the abdomen, separately mummified, and placed in four 'canopic' jars, which were then enclosed in a canopic chest. The body was dried with soda and aromatic resins for 70 days, then laid out with the hands

crossed on the chest, and wrapped in bandages. Resin was painted over the first layer of bandage, followed by the funeral jewellery of the deceased. Further bandaging followed, with linen pads or sand being inserted to fill out the human shape. The outside of the mummy was painted and gilded, and placed in a series of coffins, one outside the other.

On the day of the funeral, the coffin was placed on a sledge, which was dragged by oxen to the banks of the Nile, followed by the wailing widow and another female relation, who represented the goddesses Isis and Nephthys. After being carried by boat to the west bank of the river, the coffin was dragged to the tomb. There it was stood upright, while a priest performed a ritual intended to 'open the mouth' of the corpse, so that it could consume the food and drink being offered.

Then the coffin was lowered or carried into the burial chamber, while female mourners rent their clothing and sprinkled dust on their heads. Servants placed the canopic chest in the tomb, together with all the necessaries for life in the next world. Essential was a box containing a large number of little pottery figures. These were to take the place of the dead man if he should be asked to work in the afterlife: 'If the deceased shall be summoned to do forced labour, to plough fields or to build dikes, or to carry sand from east to west, "I will do it, here am I!" shalt thou say.'

IMPERIAL ROME

Exactly what happened on the death of a Roman citizen depended, naturally, upon his (or, to a degree, her) wealth and standing in society. Slaves and the poorest of the Romans were buried, with little or no ceremony, in a public cemetery. Those who could afford it belonged to the cooperative funeral associations – *collegia funeraticia* – who developed the extensive Roman catacombs. The wealthier families had individual tombs along the roads that led out of the city, such as those whose remains still line the Via Appia.

At the moment when a man breathed his last, his name was cried aloud – as it still is today on the death of a pope. If he failed to reply, he was judged dead. The body was washed, and dressed (provided he was entitled to it) in a toga. There was a formal acknowledgement of the death to the city authorities, and a public announcement of the forthcoming obsequies.

On the due day, the funeral procession of a rich man went first to the Forum, sometimes accompanied by actors and jesters. (There might even have been a combat of gladiators – at the funeral of Publius Licinius in AD 183, no less than 120 men fought to their deaths.) In the Forum, family and friends made speeches in praise of the deceased, and the procession then made its way through the city gates to the place of burial or cremation.

Roman law prohibited burial or cremation within the city walls, and cemeteries were not allowed near residential areas – which is why the family tombs were built along roads that led out of the city. The tombs were marked by carved stone epitaphs that included the biographical details of the dead, and sometimes a prayer, directed at passing strangers, for remembrance. There was often, also, a portrait bust. Even when cremation became common, some small part of the body, usually the bone of the little finger, was preserved symbolically.

The period of public mourning lasted nine days, at the end of which offerings were made at the tomb, and a feast was held at the deceased's home. Private mourning within the family could last for as long as a further ten months. In general, the Romans did not suppose that the spirits of

the departed left for a distant destination: rather that they coexisted among the living as ghosts, and a festival in their honour was held each year.

HINDUISM

The ceremonies surrounding death are of great importance in the Hindu religion, which is deeply influenced by doctrines concerning the soul, or *atman*, and its reincarnation (see Chapter 6). In this connection, all Hindus hope for the birth of at least one son, because only a son is able to carry out all the necessary funeral rites that will ensure the successful onward progress of the soul. These rites are usually long and complicated, and can vary according to the caste of the deceased, or the sect to which they belonged.

As death approaches, the relatives gather, and high-caste priests (known as Brahmans) are summoned. If possible, the dying individual should touch a cow, which is then presented as a gift to the most important Brahman. Both the deceased and the mourners are regarded as contaminated, and have to undergo various purification rites.

Cremation is the usual method of disposal of the body, and is performed close by a river – if possible, beside the sacred Ganges. There are strict rules concerning the treatment of the corpse, the way in which it is wrapped, and the behaviour of the funeral cortege. Equally strict rules apply to the placing of the pyre, its size, and the timber that is to be used.

*ABOVE: **The dead of the wealthy Roman families, or their ashes, were interred in the tombs that still line the Appian Way on the outskirts of what was Imperial Rome.***

*LEFT: **In the course of preparing a corpse for mummification, the internal organs were removed and preserved in separate canopic jars such as this.***

ABOVE: Many Hindus cannot afford the expense of a ritual cremation, and a dead body may often be consigned, unburnt, to the waters of the Ganges.

For many centuries, the sorrowing widow was expected to join her husband's body on the pyre, and be consumed with it. In 1829, under British rule, this custom was made illegal (see page 38), but it continued surreptitiously until very recently.

Further rules define the purification rituals that take place around the pyre, and the return home of the funeral cortege after sunset. For ten days after the funeral, the mourners are regarded as unclean, and must remain secluded. More rules dictate their behaviour during this time – for example, they must not study the Veda (the ancient sacred writings of Hinduism), or cut their hair – and every day they must perform ceremonies that are designed to enable the freed soul to find a new spiritual body. If these are not carried out, the soul may remain among the living as a ghost. The ceremonies include the setting out of milk, water, and balls of rice.

At a later date – also defined by the rules – there is a second funeral ceremony. The bones are collected from the funeral pyre and placed in containers, which are then consigned to the waters. Some sects also require a second cremation of the bones, which are ground up

RIGHT: Crumbling headstones in the medieval Old Jewish Cemetery, Prague. The stones are crowded together because the Jewish community was allocated only a small area for a cemetery, and Judaic law dictated nothing but burial for the dead.

and burnt once more. When it is time for the mourners to return to daily life, a new fire is lit in the house, but further offerings to the dead will be made at later specific dates.

JUDAISM

The Old Testament describes many of the funeral customs of the early Jews – rending of garments, self-mutilation – but these were taken over from more ancient peoples, and some were later prohibited by law as being pagan. The book of Leviticus states, 'Ye shall not make any cuttings in your flesh for the dead, nor print any marks upon you'; and Deuteronomy lays down, 'Ye shall not cut yourselves, nor make any baldness between your eyes for the dead.' Burial was the usual custom, if possible in the home country, and 'with one's fathers'. Deprivation of proper burial was a disgrace, and ritual lamentation became almost as important as the funeral itself.

Modern Judaism has preserved many of its ancient customs, but the most important aspect of a Jewish funeral is its simplicity. As death approaches, the dying person confesses his or her sins, and declares the *Shema*, 'Hear, O Israel, the Lord our God, the Lord is One'. The dead body is laid on the ground, and psalms are recited – particularly psalm 91, 'He that dwelleth in the secret place of the most High shall abide under the shadow of the Almighty. I will say of the Lord, He is my refuge and my fortress; my God; in him will I trust…' Then the body is washed, and wrapped in a white linen shroud.

In many cases, the washing of the corpse, and the funeral ceremony, is supervised by members of voluntary or professional organizations known as 'holy brotherhoods'. The body is placed in an inexpensive wooden coffin, possibly just four plain boards loosely joined together, or consigned directly to the earth in its shroud, and a handful of dust from Israel is placed in the grave or the coffin. The service consists of psalms, speeches in praise of the departed, prayers for the repose of the soul, and the final recital of the *Kaddish*, a hymn of praise to God.

On their return from the funeral, the mourners eat a simple meal prepared for them by friends or neighbours. In orthodox families, the next of kin tear their upper garments, and remain indoors for seven days (the *shivah*), sitting on low stools. Mourning may continue for a month, or for a year; these stages of the return of the mourners to normal life are supposed to reflect the soul's gradual progress to the afterlife.

ISLAM

There are certain similarities between the prayers recited at Islamic and at Jewish deathbeds. A dying Muslim declares his faith, 'There is no God but Allah, and Mahomed is his true prophet', and *sura* 36 of the Koran – which concerns the last judgment – is recited over the dead body.

The corpse is then laid on a stretcher, directed toward Mecca, and reverently washed according to exact rules. The eyes are closed, and the feet are tied together. The body's orifices are stuffed with cotton, and the corpse is sprinkled with rose water and camphor. Then it is wrapped in several shrouds – always an odd number, but how many, and their colour, is a matter of varying practice. Following this, the *salat aldjinaza* – a prayer for the dead – is recited. Usually, there is a watch over the dead body, and men may be hired to recite appropriate sections of the Koran.

The funeral follows very soon after – if possible, within 24 hours. The bier supporting the body – whether that of a man or a woman – is borne only by men. It is considered meritable to follow the procession – and on foot, because the angels of death always go on foot – and particularly to help carry the bier for forty paces.

The grave is quite deep, sufficiently so to allow room for the deceased to sit up, because it is believed that he or she will subsequently be examined for orthodoxy by the angels Munkar and Nakir. The body is laid on its right side, with the face toward Mecca. There is very little further ritual. A shawl is torn, three handfuls of soil are thrown into the grave by the mourners, and *sura* 112 of the Koran is recited. In many cases, the correct answers to the catechism that the deceased will later undergo are whispered into his ear by two *fiqis* (tutors). Then the tomb is closed.

LEFT: Jewish women bewail the death of an Israeli soldier.

BELOW: A Muslim funeral procession in Zinjiang Province, China. The bier is borne only by men, and it is considered particularly meritorious to help carry it for forty paces.

On the night following the burial, Munkar and Nakir are said to enter the tomb to question the deceased on his faith. If they get the right answers, they open the side of the tomb so that he can view the Paradise awaiting him. If they do not, they beat him, and the deceased's torment continues until the end of the world.

Strict Islamic ritual disapproves of wailing, speeches in praise of the dead, or the ornamenting of the tomb and placing of inscriptions; however, all of these frequently take place. On the return home, the fiqis may hold a funeral repast, and recite the *sabha* – the rosary of the 1000 beads.

Islamic law requires friends and neighbours to pay visits of condolence to the bereaved, and the women wail every Thursday for three weeks, while on Fridays they go to the grave. These visits may continue for some time.

CHRISTIANITY

Mourning for the dead was not a part of early Christian funeral rites, because the deceased was believed to have ascended to join the Lord, and await the final resurrection. So funerals were considered occasions for rejoicing, and the bereaved wore white clothing. By the eighth century, however, fear of what happened after death had crept into Christian belief: the

Even in the midst of life we are in death. Black-clad mourners walk past a field of flourishing wild flowers on their way to church for a funeral in Romania.

mourners wore black, and prayers were said for the deliverance of the soul. By the late Middle Ages, the modern form of death ritual had developed.

Christian rites vary considerably according to the branch of the Catholic Church – Roman, Greek or Russian – and equally among the many Protestant sects, but there are basic similarities. Protestant rites are usually a modified and simplified version derived from the Catholic rites that preceded them.

At the approach of the death of a Roman Catholic, a priest is summoned to hear confession and absolve the dying person, to administer Holy Communion and then extreme unction – anointing with oil that has been blessed by a bishop. The burial, also in the presence of a priest, is preceded by prayers for the dead, and on the day of the funeral some form of requiem will be recited, and the body in its coffin will be blessed with incense and sprinkled with holy water.

Dying Protestants may ask for their pastor to attend the deathbed, when prayers will be said. It is still customary for a brief prayer for the departed to be included in the parish service on the Sunday following the death. The funeral service itself can take many forms, and may include speeches and readings by relatives and close friends.

Quaker funerals are, like other Quaker meetings, quiet and relatively informal occasions. One or more of those present will be expected to speak personally about the deceased, others might be moved to read out or quote some appropriate words, but much of the time may be taken up by silent contemplation. Thereafter, the body may be buried with a simple ceremony, or cremated at a municipal crematorium.

Greek Orthodox burials last, in the first instance, for only three to five years. After this, the body is exhumed in a family ceremony, with a priest in attendance. The bones are washed, sometimes in wine, left to dry in the sun, put into a casket and placed in a columbarium – so called because it is a building fitted with niches that looks rather like a dovecote (from the Latin *columba* – a dove).

BUDDHISM

As in the Christian world, there are many variations in funeral rituals among Buddhists, depending on local beliefs. The most usual method of disposal of the body is by cremation, although burial, embalming, or even exposure to the elements, are also practised. Sometimes the dead body is kept buried or embalmed for a considerable period before cremation.

Buddhism lays great importance on proper preparation for death on the part of the dying person. Death is not an end, but the beginning of a new existence. Only the truly enlightened can expect to be released from another existence, and enter the state of Nirvana (see page 101). So the final meditation of the dying will determine the nature of their rebirth.

However, many common funeral rites represent the efforts of the survivors to improve the subsequent fate of the deceased. Popular superstition is concerned with a fear of hell and vindictive demons: meritorious acts are performed on behalf of the dead in the hope of reducing their punishment, and mantras are recited to invoke mercy. Among certain sects, after ritual washing, the corpse is ordained as a monk, in order to ensure his worthiness. There is often some form of wake, and possibly an elaborate temple ritual, which involves the burning of incense, a declaration of the faith, and an invocation of the Buddha and his associated gods.

In China and Japan, where the religion derived from various kinds of Buddhism, it is still customary for the mourners to dress in white. A nineteenth-century book called *The Faiths of the World* describes a Japanese funeral:

The body, after being carefully washed by a favourite servant, and the head shaved, is clothed according to the state of the weather, and (if a female, in her best apparel) exactly as in life, except that the sash is tied, not in a bow, but strongly fastened with two knots, to indicate that it is nevermore to be loosed. The body is then covered with a piece of linen, folded in a peculiar manner, and is placed on a mat in the middle of the hall, the head to the north. Food is offered to it, and all the family lament.

After being kept for forty-eight hours, the body is placed on its knees in a tub-shaped coffin, which is enclosed in a square, oblong box, or bier, the top of which is roof-shaped, called quan…

The quan, followed by the eldest son and the family, servants, friends and acquaintances, is borne in procession, with flags, lanterns, etc, to one of the neighbouring temples, whence, after certain ceremonies, in which the priests take a leading part, it is carried, by the relatives only, to the grave… The moment they are come, the tub containing the body is taken out of the quan and deposited in the grave, which is then filled with earth and covered with a flat stone, which again is covered with earth, and over the whole is placed the quan…

If the deceased had preferred to be burnt, the quan is taken to the summit of one of two neighbouring mountains, on the top of each of which is a sort of furnace, prepared

Dressed from head to foot in white, three women follow a Chinese funeral in Macao.

*RIGHT: **Preparation for a mountainside cremation in Nepal. Priests and mourners look on as the body is washed behind the privacy of a large cloth.***

for this purpose, enclosed in a small hut. The coffin is then taken from the quan and, being placed in the furnace, a great fire is kindled. The eldest son is provided with an earthen urn, in which first the bones and then the ashes are put, after which the mouth of the urn is sealed up. While the body is burning, a priest recites hymns. The urn is then carried to the grave, and deposited in it, and, the grave being filled up, the quan is placed over it.

The eldest son and his brothers are dressed in white, in garments of undyed hempen stuff, as are the bearers, and all females attending the funeral, whether relatives or not... The eldest son and heir, whether by blood or adoption, wears also a broad-brimmed hat, of rushes, which hang about his shoulders, and in this attire does not recognise nor salute anybody.

The same work also describes Chinese funeral rites:

As soon as an individual dies, his body is enclosed in an airtight coffin, and kept for seven weeks in the house, in the course of which time every fourth day is devoted to special funeral ceremonies. Food is offered to the dead body... and prayers are put up by Buddhist and Taoist priests... Women are the principal mourners among the Chinese, and it is often a most affecting sight to see them kneeling and howling in lonely burial-grounds, by the graves of their husbands and children.

Their places of burial are in barren hills and mountain sides, but sometimes vaults are preferred: great numbers of dead bodies are placed in plank coffins, and retained above ground for many years. The deceased members of the same family may sometimes be seen laid side by side in open sheds to the amount of fifteen or twenty. The Buddhist priests burn the bodies of their dead and place them in common vaults.

In Tibet, the *Bardo Thödol*, the so-called 'book of the dead', plays an important part in funerary ritual. Traditionally, it is recited at the side of the deathbed by a lama, and its purpose is to prepare the dying person for the nightmare experiences to come in the 49 days between death and rebirth (see page 167).

It is important that the dying individual should remain conscious for as long as possible during the reading. With this end in view, they are turned over on to their right side, in the yogic pose known as the 'lion position', and the arteries of the neck are massaged to prevent loss of consciousness.

After death has occurred, the face is covered with a white cloth, and the door and windows

*BELOW: **Dressed in white, as the custom dictates, mourners are led through the streets at a Chinese funeral.***

are covered up. The lama positions himself by the head, studying it to determine when the life principle has finally departed from the body. This may take from 12 hours to four days. An astrologer draws up a horoscope for the moment of death, which provides advice on the appropriate funeral rites, and the means of disposal of the body.

After this period, the body is seated in a corner of the room, and relatives are summoned for a funeral feast, which may last two days, during which food and drink are offered to the corpse. Then the body is cremated, or left exposed on the mountainside. A wooden effigy of the deceased is dressed in his or her clothes, and for the rest of the 49 days lamas chant various liturgies before it. Finally, the effigy is decorated and dismembered.

AFRICA

Unlike the major religions, traditional African religions have no sacred texts which lay down beliefs and rituals. So everything is passed on through tribal elders, by word of mouth, from one generation to the next. As a result, even within a single political region, there may be hundreds of varying religious traditions.

Anthropologists divide traditional societies into two types: hunter-gatherers and agricultural societies. Hunter-gatherers appear to take death as a matter of course, with little or no concept of an afterlife. Concerning the Hazda people of northern Tanzania, one anthropologist noted:

There is no period of mourning involving a second phase of rites, and the deceased's possessions are immediately shared without ceremony... Death is thought to have neither social nor supernatural consequences for the living... The social and spiritual existence of the person ends with the burial of the corpse.

Mourners comfort a young chief's widow as she weeps at his funeral in Ethiopia. She wears her husband's gunbelt.

Agricultural societies, on the other hand, are likely to have ancestor cults (see page 113), and a defined view of an afterlife. They make no sharp distinction between life and death, and death is seen as only a change in status: the dead remain a real presence within the community. They are therefore buried with suitable rites, and food, clothes and cooking pots are provided for their continued existence.

CHRISTIAN CREMATION

AGRICULTURAL SOCIETIES...MAKE

NO SHARP DISTINCTION BETWEEN

LIFE AND DEATH, AND DEATH IS

SEEN ONLY AS A CHANGE IN STATUS:

THE DEAD REMAIN A REAL

PRESENCE IN THE COMMUNITY

For centuries, most Christians objected to cremation on the grounds that it invalidated the doctrine of the resurrection of the body (see page 107), and many Catholics still hold this view. Until the late nineteenth century, cremation was illegal in Europe, and the ban on Roman Catholic cremation was not lifted until 1964.

As early as the seventeenth century, however, the English physician and writer Sir Thomas Browne (1605–82) wrote: 'To be knaved out of our graves, to have our skulls made drinking-bowls, and our bones turned into Pipes, to delight and Sport our Enemies, are Tragical abominations escaped in burning Burials.'

71

RIGHT: *The serious danger to health of overcrowded cemeteries is exemplified in this notice prohibiting any further burials, in the churchyards of Dudley, Staffordshire, of those who had died of cholera during the epidemic of 1832.*

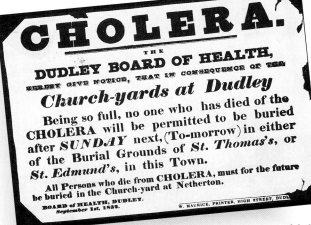

CHOLERA.

DUDLEY BOARD OF HEALTH,

HEREBY GIVE NOTICE, THAT IN CONSEQUENCE OF THE

Church-yards at Dudley

Being so full, no one who has died of the CHOLERA will be permitted to be buried after *SUNDAY* next, (To-morrow) in either of the Burial Grounds of St. Thomas's, or St. Edmund's, in this Town.

All Persons who die from CHOLERA, must for the future be buried in the Church-yard at Netherton.

BOARD of HEALTH, DUDLEY.
September 1st, 1832.

W. MAURICE, PRINTER, HIGH STREET, DUDL

During the nineteenth century, many people became disturbed by the sanitation problems caused by drainage from churchyards and cemeteries, and by their increasing demands on land. In 1843, the English reformer Sir Edwin Chadwick published a book entitled *A Special Inquiry into the Practice of Interment in Towns*. In 1874, a congress of physicians and chemists in Milan, Italy, petitioned the Chamber of Deputies for a clause permitting cremation. In the same year, the Cremation Society of England was founded.

The founder of the society was the royal surgeon Sir Henry Thompson (1820–1904). He maintained that the aim of cremation was a simple one:

'Given a dead body, to resolve it into carbonic acid, water and ammonia, rapidly, safely, and not unpleasantly'. The Cremation Society declared, 'We disapprove of the present custom of burying the dead, and desire to substitute some mode which shall rapidly resolve the body into its component elements by a process which cannot offend the living, and shall render the remains absolutely innocuous. Until some better method is devised, we desire to adopt that usually known as cremation'.

Many legal obstacles were placed in the society's way. They were unable to obtain any freehold land until 1878, when they succeeded in purchasing an acre at Woking in Surrey. In 1882, two persons died, leaving express instructions that they were to be cremated there.

An application was made to the Home Secretary, but permission was refused, and the bodies were preserved until a member of the society built a crematorium on his estate in Dorset, where they were finally cremated. A year later he himself died, and was also cremated.

The Home Office took no action at the time. But in 1884 a Dr William Price of Llantrisant, Glamorgan, announced publicly that he intended to cremate the body of his 5-month-old baby son. Dr Price claimed to be an arch-druid, performing rites while dressed in a white tunic and a head-dress made of fox skin. He opposed vaccination, and practised 'free love',

RIGHT: **Dr William Price claimed to be an arch-druid, and performed archaic rituals wearing a head-dress of fox skin. In 1884 he cremated the body of his 5-month-old baby son. He was tried at Cardiff Assizes, but the judge declared the cremation to be legal.**

and the infant, who was born when Price was 83, was christened Jesus Christ. After Price had cremated the boy, his arrest was ordered, and he was tried at Cardiff Assizes. However, the judge ruled that no offence had taken place, and that cremation was legal. In 1885, the first controlled cremation took place at the Cremation Society's site in Woking, and Price himself was cremated there in 1893.

The first crematorium in the United States was built in 1876 by Dr Julius Lemoyne. A number of cremation societies were founded during the 1880s, and by 1900 there were 24 crematoriums in America, and more than 13,000 people had been cremated. Finally, the Cremation Association of America was established in 1913. By the early twentieth century, cremation was legal in most countries.

Many people do not appreciate the extremely high temperatures necessary to reduce a corpse to ashes – murderers who attempt to dispose of a body by burning are seldom successful. Crematoria make use of a furnace – generally fired by oil, natural gas or electricity – which recirculates the hot gases, and which can attain temperatures of up to 1,500°C (2,732°F). Before the body is burned, it must be stripped of all clothing, jewellery, dental bridges, prostheses, and any other devices such as heart pacemakers. It is then wrapped in a sheet of paper or some other inflammable material.

In typical crematorium conditions, an average body can be consumed in two to three hours, leaving between 6 and 12 pounds (3 to 5.5 kilograms) of ashes and bone fragments. After the furnace has cooled, any remaining traces of metal are removed with a magnet, and the 'cremains' are ground to a fine powder. These may be returned to the family in a cardboard carton, or similar temporary container. Later they can be enshrined or buried in a space much smaller than that required for a coffin. In a French report of 1973, it was calculated that, in a single year, cremation in Great Britain had saved an area of ground equal to 607 football fields.

The ultimate fate of the ashes can take many different forms. Some people wish their remains to be scattered in places they loved while alive. Packets of the ashes of American labour leader Joe Hill, who died in 1915, were delivered to local chapters of the Industrial Workers of the World (the 'Wobblies'), and to unions all over the globe. Members of a cremation society in San Diego, California, have requested that their ashes should – illegally – be put into the garbage, or flushed down the drain.

The remains of Cazimir Liszinski, burned as a heretic in Poland in 1689, were fired from a cannon – an example followed more recently, when remains have been packed into cartridges or fireworks. A nineteenth-century Frenchman, the Abbé François-Valentine, suggested that ash and bones could be used to make glass medallions. One man had his ashes mixed with paints, which were used in a posthumous portrait for his family. And, not long ago, a Florida widower had his dead wife's ashes put into capsules, one of which he swallowed each day.

> IN TYPICAL CREMATORIUM CONDITIONS, AN AVERAGE BODY CAN BE CONSUMED IN TWO TO THREE HOURS, LEAVING BETWEEN 6 AND 12 POUNDS OF ASHES AND BONE FRAGMENTS

Modern crematoria are provided with automated machinery for transferring the body to the furnace, avoiding any manual handling.

in New Mexico. On the way, the ashes were twice mislaid, once forgotten on a railway platform, and there was even a plot among some of Lawrence's friends to steal them, and scatter them to the winds. There is considerable doubt about the eventual fate of the ashes: according to some reports, they were interred at Taos; other versions have them mixed with cement to make a mantelshelf in the ranch-house.

In 1943, the ashes of American journalist Alexander Woollcott were sent by mail to be interred at Hamilton College, New York State, but were delivered by mistake to Colgate University. They were redirected, and eventually arrived at Hamilton – with 67 cents postage due.

Errors of another kind can also occur, one that this epitaph found in a graveyard at Cardington, Ohio, witnesses:

My husband promised me
That my body should be
Cremated but other
Influences prevailed

BURIED ALIVE?

One of the objections raised to cremation was the fear that a person could be wrongly pronounced dead (see Chapter 1), and burnt while still alive. This fear applied equally to premature burial, which became an obsession with many people during the nineteenth century. Many books were written on the subject. One of these, by a certain Franz Hartmann, appeared in 1895. It cited the evidence of more than 700 alleged cases of premature burial: hissing noises from coffins or vaults, bodies that had moved after interment, torn shrouds, wood splinters discovered under the fingernails – presumably due to frantic attempts to break out of the coffin – and even pregnant women who had given birth after burial.

The *British Medical Journal* gave the book a dismissive review in 1896, but the fear remained. In that same year a Russian Doctor of the Law Faculty at the University of Louvain, Count Karnice-Karnicki, invented an ingenious device. It was basically a tube that passed down into the coffin and attached to the chest of the corpse. The slightest movement of the chest wall caused

There is some doubt as to the eventual fate of the ashes of the English writer D.H. Lawrence, but this small chapel on the ranch near Taos, New Mexico, where he spent time between 1922 and 1925, is reputed to contain them.

There have, of course, been many mistakes. The Neptune Society of Los Angeles handed over ashes to a widow whose husband's body was discovered four months later in a mortuary refrigerator. A woman in Florida discovered a pair of dentures in what were said to be her husband's ashes – he did not wear any. She learnt that his true ashes had been scattered at sea, against his express wishes, and was awarded half a million dollars in damages.

The English writer D.H. Lawrence died in 1930 at a sanatorium near Antibes in France. In 1935 his body was exhumed and cremated, and his ashes were carried to America by Angelo Ravagli, who was then the lover of Lawrence's widow, Frieda. It was her intention to place them in a chapel, built by Ravagli, on a ranch at Taos

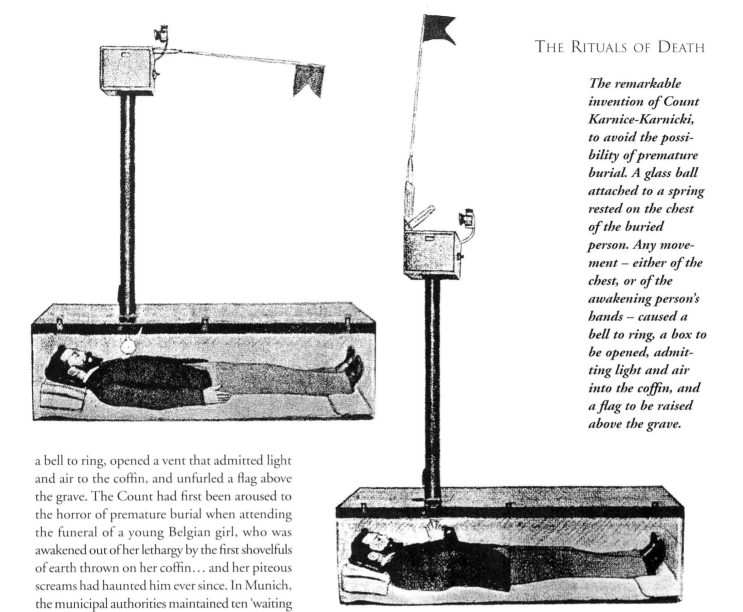

a bell to ring, opened a vent that admitted light and air to the coffin, and unfurled a flag above the grave. The Count had first been aroused to the horror of premature burial when attending the funeral of a young Belgian girl, who was awakened out of her lethargy by the first shovelfuls of earth thrown on her coffin… and her piteous screams had haunted him ever since. In Munich, the municipal authorities maintained ten 'waiting mortuaries', where the dead were kept for three days after death had been pronounced. Their fingers were attached to a complicated system of cords and pulleys, any movement of which made a bell ring in the porter's lodge.

Some people took different precautions, requesting that their arteries should be severed before they were buried. And when the antiquarian Francis Douce died in 1834, his will was found to contain the following bequest, 'I give to Sir Anthony Carlisle [a distinguished surgeon] two hundred pounds, requesting him to sever my head or extract my heart from my body, so as to prevent any possibility of the return of vitality.'

In America in the late nineteenth and early twentieth centuries, the fear of premature burial was allayed by the growing practice of embalming. Once the body had been subjected to this radical treatment, there was no question of its survival.

LAST RESPECTS

When somebody dies, the survivors are frequently left with a sense of guilt. Did they show sufficient love or devotion while the deceased was still alive? Deep down, do they feel that life could have been saved by some proper form of ceremony? It is this feeling, independent of any atavistic motivation, that lies, in part, behind the need for people to pay their 'last respects' before a funeral.

Even at a domestic level, the viewing of the corpse in its coffin – or, indeed, the physical presence of the corpse at a wake – is an open demonstration of this need. When the dead person is known – from reputation, or via the images of film and television – not just to family and friends, but to thousands or even millions,

At the centre of a double file of honour guards, the coffin of Eva Peron, wife of the Argentinian dictator, is carried on a gun carriage. At her lying-in-state in 1952, more than 20 people were killed in the crush, and some 4,500 were injured.

some means must be found to allow a mass expression of respect, of shock, even of grief.

So, when a national or international celebrity dies arrangements have to be made for the body to lie in state. When this occurs it is important for the crowds who come to view it to be kept under control. This can present serious problems for the authorities.

More than 300,000 people crowded into New York City Hall in 1885 to view the body of US President Ulysses S. Grant as it lay in state, and over 300 policemen struggled to control them. Even 'Buffalo Bill' Cody drew 25,000 to the Colorado State Capitol in 1917. In this case, order was maintained by a tophatted ringmaster with a cane, who called out repeatedly, 'Step lively please, a big crowd's behind. Hurry up folks.'

When the silent film star Rudolph Valentino died in the United States in 1926, there were hysterical scenes – and even several suicides. His body was exhibited in a glass-sided casket in Frank Campbell's Funeral Church on Broadway, New York, and very soon a crowd estimated at 80,000 had completely blocked traffic movement, and 250 police officers were attempting, unsuccessfully, to control them. Within the first hour, the funeral home had been stripped of anything that might be considered a souvenir; windows were shattered, furniture was shredded, cars overturned, and hundreds of people trampled to the ground. Eventually, more than 90,000 people edged past the casket, afforded, at most, a three-second glimpse of their dead hero.

There were reported to be more than 20 deaths, and 4,500 injured, during the lying in state in 1952 of Eva Perón, wife of the Argentinian dictator. Between two and three million queued for as much as 16 hours – six abreast in a line extending for 30 city blocks – to touch the casket and kiss the glass.

And, when Elvis Presley died in Memphis in 1977, as writer Malcolm Forbes described in his book, *They Went That-A-Way*:

Within an hour of the announcement of his death that afternoon, more than 1,000 people crowded around the gates of Graceland. By the next day, when Elvis's reconstructed, post-autopsied body was laid out in his mansion, some 80,000 had made the pilgrimage. Hundreds fainted, one man had a heart attack, a woman went into labour, and the National Guard was called out.

Other lyings in state have been attended with greater solemnity – and fewer casualties. In England, the custom of displaying the body of a dead king began with Henry II in 1189. The body of Edward VII was viewed by half-a-million people in Westminster Hall in 1910. Over 800,000 queued to see the body of George V, displayed in the same venue for four days in 1936.

American presidents usually lie in state in the Capitol in Washington, DC. James Garfield, who was assassinated in 1881, drew a crowd of 150,000 in two days.

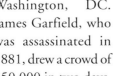

When Herbert Hoover lay there in 1964, mourners passed by at a calculated 2,500 per hour. John F. Kennedy, assassinated in 1963, lay in a closed casket; nevertheless, 250,000 filed by to pay their last respects.

French author Victor Hugo was laid in state under the Arc de Triomphe in Paris in 1884, and his funeral cortege was followed to the Pantheon by two million admirers. The record, however, must be held by Abraham Lincoln. More than seven million Americans saw the body of the assassinated president as the funeral train travelled slowly from Washington to his burial place in Springfield, Illinois. At each stop – Baltimore, Harrisburg, Philadelphia, New York, Albany, Buffalo, Cleveland, Columbus, Indianapolis and Chicago – the coffin was opened to reveal Lincoln's face to many thousands, and in Springfield it was displayed for 24 hours to a further 75,000.

State funerals are generally very lavish affairs, attended with much pomp and ceremony. There are honour guards drawn from the armed forces, solemn music, and a cortege including heads of state from other countries. There are, however, exceptions. When the President of France, Charles de Gaulle, died in 1970, his body was placed in a plain wooden coffin made by a local carpenter, and buried in the small village cemetery of Colombey-les-Deux-Eglises, attended only by his family, friends and neighbours.

The locomotive that drew Abraham Lincoln's corpse from Washington DC to Springfield, Illinois. More than seven million Americans are said to have viewed the dead president's body.

CHAPTER 5

IN MEMORIAM

From earliest times, it has frequently been the custom to raise a marker of some kind over the grave of a dead person. In those cultures where the dead are believed to remain in spirit close to the society in which they have lived, this may be regarded as a kind of 'house', and as such it was often provided with domestic necessities. As belief in an afterlife developed, these necessities came to be thought of rather as things required during the journey the deceased was to take from this world to the next. Food and drink was provided, favourite pets or horses, servants, sometimes a chariot or carriage, or – among seagoing peoples – a ship. A tomb big enough to contain all these, or even a ship or ship-shaped grave, had to be constructed.

LASTING MEMORIALS

Without doubt, it was the ancient Egyptians who erected the largest memorial tombs. At first – about 3000 BC – their burials were made in subterranean chambers, with only a small structure above ground to mark their position. This structure gradually developed into a low, flat-roofed building, built of mud bricks, now called a mastaba – which means 'bench' in Arabic. The inner walls carried paintings and reliefs that represented the deceased enjoying his favourite occupations, and his servants at their daily work.

The pharaoh Zoser was the first to commission a mastaba entirely of stone. It was built at Saqqara near Memphis, in 2680 BC. It was about 8 metres (26 feet) high and square in ground plan, with sides some 63 metres (207 feet) long. This building was then extended on the ground, until each side measured over 100 metres (328 feet), and a further five terraces, of diminishing size, were built on top, to reach a height of 60 metres (197 feet). Known as the Step Pyramid, this is the earliest building of its kind in Egypt. Inside, there is a complicated system of corridors and rooms, with a central shaft 25 metres (82 feet) deep and 8 metres (26 feet) wide, at the bottom of which is the burial chamber. Still standing today, the building is surrounded by a huge walled court.

A century later, the pharaoh Snefru ordered the building of a similar structure, at Dahshur, a little south of Saqqara. It is 188 metres square (2,000 square feet) at the base, and some 98

*FACING PAGE: **In Mexico, the dead are welcomed back temporarily to the land of the living in the first days of November. Skeletal figures of all kinds can be seen in the streets and in the cities – even riding the trams and buses.***

*LEFT: **The first memorial pyramid in Egypt was the five-stepped mastaba erected on the orders of the pharaoh Zoser in 2680 BC. It rises to a height of 60 metres (197 feet).***

*ABOVE: **The largest earth mound in Europe is Silbury Hill in Wiltshire, of approximately the same date as the pyramid of Zoser. Tradition says that a great British king is buried at its heart.***

*ABOVE RIGHT: **The interior of West Kennet Long Barrow – also in Wiltshire – which contains stone chambers that accommodated the skeletons of 40 people.***

metres (321 feet) high. It is unusual in that the slope of the lower half is steeper than that of the upper half. Snefru also raised another structure at Maydum, which is now considered to be the first true pyramid. The early building was a small step pyramid, which was enlarged until it was eight terraces high. Then the steps were filled in with stone, and covered with a smooth slope of limestone. The pharaoh Snefru is also believed to have commissioned another pyramid at Dahshur. Some 220 metres (722 feet) at the base, and 104 metres (340 feet) high, it is nearly as large as the pyramids at Giza.

These three great pyramids stand on a plateau a few miles outside Cairo. The largest

THE GREAT PYRAMID IN EGYPT WAS ORIGINALLY 230 METRES SQUARE (2,475 SQUARE FEET) AND NEARLY 147 METRES (480 FEET) HIGH. IT HAS BEEN CALCULATED THAT ST PETER'S IN ROME, THE CATHEDRALS OF BOTH FLORENCE AND MILAN, WESMINSTER ABBEY AND ST PAUL'S CATHEDRAL COULD ALL STAND INSIDE IT

and oldest of these is known as the Great Pyramid, and was erected in about 2528 BC by the pharaoh Khufu (sometimes known as Cheops), Snefru's son and successor. It was originally 230 metres square (2,475 square feet), and nearly 147 metres (480 feet) high – it has been calculated that St Peter's in Rome, the cathedrals of both Florence and Milan, Westminster Abbey and St Paul's Cathedral could all stand inside its area. Although there is a central chamber known as the King's Chamber, which contains a bare red granite sarcophagus, there is no evidence that Khufu was ever interred there.

In later centuries, Egyptian tombs were usually a series of chambers cut into the rock of a hillside. Carved effigies of the deceased and his wife occupied the innermost chamber. Some small pyramid tombs for private persons were also built. They stood 3 to 4 metres (10 to 13 feet) high, and the chamber containing the coffin took up most of the interior. In the eighth century BC, Egypt was conquered by people coming northward from the Sudan. Their kings had pyramid tombs built for themselves in their homeland. The last of these Sudanese pyramids, dating from the third and fourth centuries AD, are relatively small brick buildings.

Almost rivalling the pyramids in some cases, though of an earlier age and much simpler construction, are the earth mounds raised in Europe by the Neolithic and early Bronze Age peoples as much as 10,000 years ago. The biggest of these is Silbury Hill in Wiltshire, which is 40 metres (131 feet) high and dates from 2600 BC. Tradition maintains that a great king is buried at its heart, but investigation has so far revealed no evidence at all to support the claim.

Many smaller mounds – known in English as 'barrows' – were built of earth over tombs of huge stones or 'megaliths'. The West Kennet Long Barrow, close by Silbury Hill, is 100 metres (328 feet) long, and contains stone chambers that accommodated the skeletons of 40 people. There are thousands of constructions of this type to be found in the British Isles, Brittany and Scandinavia, not all of them burial sites. Many have been stripped of their earth covering, either by man or by weather, leaving only the bare stone framework standing.

Similar burial mounds were constructed by the inhabitants of east-central North America, particularly in the valleys of the Ohio and Mississippi rivers, during the period 1000 BC to AD 700. Further north, around the Great Lakes, mounds have been found in the shape of animals, birds and other figures. Many of these have not been excavated, so it is not known whether they are burial sites or not.

Strangely similar to the European mounds are the 'stupas' of Buddhist countries. Asoka, the Emperor of India (274–232 BC), is said to have gathered all the relics of Buddha he could lay his hands on, and distributed them to 84,000 sites throughout his lands. The stupas, monumental memorial tombs, were erected to

LEFT: The ancient Greeks erected steles – upright slabs with the representation of a face, and an inscription – to commemorate their dead.

LEFT: Burial mounds, very similar to those raised in Europe, are found in North America, particularly in the valleys of the Ohio and Mississippi rivers. They were built between 1000 BC and AD 700. Close to this mound at Marietta, Ohio, are the graves of nineteenth-century settlers.

house the relics, but only a few remain. The great stone stupa at Sanchi, a small village in central Madhya Pradesh, one of three surviving built by Asoka, is 32 metres (105 feet) in diameter, and 13 metres (42 feet) high. In Sri Lanka, King Duttha-gamani raised a stupa – known as the 'gold dust' dagaba – to house the sacred footprint of Buddha. Built of brick, it is 88 metres (289 feet) in diameter, and 81 metres (266 feet) high.

In Japan, tomb mounds were raised between the third and sixth centuries AD. Built to accommodate the bodies of royalty and members of the aristocracy, they have a keyhole shape, and are surrounded by moats. Some are huge: the burial site of fourth-century Emperor Nintoku, near Osaka, is 486 metres (1594 feet) long, and 35 metres (115 feet) high.

The earliest known memorial tablets to individuals are the stone steles discovered in Mesopotamia, such as that of Hammurabi, which dates from 1680 BC, and which is now in the Louvre in Paris. From about the sixth century BC, the Greeks also commemorated their dead with steles – upright slabs of stone that were painted or carved. At first these showed the figure of the deceased. Later, they included scenes from their lives. For example, the stele of Hegeso shows her choosing jewellery from a box held by her servant; while, on the stele of Dexileos, a young cavalryman killed in 394 BC, he is represented killing an enemy soldier.

In time, the Greek rulers began to commission enormous memorials to themselves. At Halicarnassus, huge figures of King Mausolus and his queen in a chariot top a colossal monument, providing the root from which comes the word 'mausoleum'. Soon, all the great

> THE EARLIEST KNOWN MEMORIAL TABLETS TO INDIVIDUALS ARE THE STONE STELES DISCOVERED IN MESOPOTAMIA, WHICH DATE FROM 1680 BC

*BELOW: **The tombs at Petra, in Jordan, are carved out of the surrounding cliffs. This so-called 'treasury of the Pharaohs' is a three-chambered royal tomb.***

*ABOVE: **The burial sites in the Roman Jewish catacombs are marked by a simple seven- or nine-branched** menorah.*

Greek cities – such as Alexandria, Antioch, Pergamum and Ephesus – were dotted with similar memorials to their rulers.

Further east, in the south of the kingdom of Jordan, almost all that remains of the Nabataean city of Petra is tombs. The so-called 'treasury of the Pharaoh' is a three-chambered king's tomb, with a remarkable classical facade, pillars and pediments two storeys high, carved entirely out of the face of the rock.

In Rome, the richer people were buried, or their ashes preserved, in private family tombs. These were often imposing structures, sometimes with a portrait relief or bust, and suitable inscriptions (see page 89).

Although subsequently a place of Christian burial, the famous subterranean catacombs of Rome were probably first excavated by the Jewish population of the city. The wide plain surrounding Rome is made up of volcanic strata, and one of these, granular tufa, is relatively easy to dig, and porous so that it drains easily, but at the same time is strong enough to support chambers and galleries.

Graves in the early Jewish catacombs were marked simply by a seven- or nine-branched *menorah* (candelabrum). In the Christian catacombs, bodies were at first placed in small rooms opening off the galleries. Later, as the number of dead increased, grave niches were cut in the walls of the galleries, sometimes as many as twelve high, and eventually even the floors

ABOVE: ***Père-Lachaise Cemetery in Paris was opened in 1803. It contains the graves of many eminent people.***

ABOVE: ***The memorial to Abraham Lincoln in Washington DC is an outstanding example of the revived classical style. It was built between 1914 and 1922.***

were used. The principal decorations of these chambers and galleries are frescoes representing scenes from the Old and New Testaments. Individuals are indicated by memorial slabs bearing relatively brief inscriptions, usually in Greek, such as, 'In thy prayers pray for us, for we know that thou dwellest in Christ.'

With the establishment of Christianity throughout Europe, burial came back into favour, and for most people the marking of graves continued to be very simple. Only very eminent people were honoured with a tomb, usually in a church, abbey or cathedral.

It was during the Renaissance that memorial monuments began to return to the classical style. Leonardo da Vinci (1452–1519) designed a magnificent tomb for Gian Giacomo Trivulzio, the ruler of Milan. It was never built, but Leonardo's preliminary drawings survive – on top of the massive base, there was to be a life-

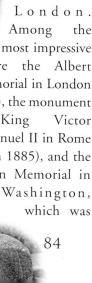

RIGHT: *The decoration of modern tombs can take many bizarre forms in celebration of the past of the dead. Here an Air Madagascar airliner tops this tomb in southern Malagasy.*

BELOW: *During the nineteenth century, funerary monuments became very elaborate, frequently representing angels or figures of mourning.*

size figure of Trivulzio, mounted on a horse that reared over a crouching adversary.

Another tomb that was not completed was that designed in 1505 by Michelangelo (1475–1564) for pope Julius II. This was to have 47 standing figures surrounding a huge statue of the pontiff himself. Later, Michelangelo realized his monumental ambitions in the memorial to Giuliano and Lorenzo de' Medici in their chapel in San Lorenzo, Florence.

Michelangelo's example was soon followed, first by Bernini (1598–1680) in Rome, and later throughout Europe. Memorial statues to rulers and great leaders are now to be found in all major cities, although few mark the position of the actual burial – the twentieth-century monument to Karl Marx in Highgate Cemetery, London, being an exception. Many take the classical form of a column or obelisk, such as the Washington Obelisk in Washington, DC, or Nelson's Column in London. Among the most impressive are the Albert Memorial in London (1872), the monument to King Victor Emmanuel II in Rome (begun 1885), and the Lincoln Memorial in Washington, which was built between 1914 and 1922.

During the nineteenth century there was also a return to the practice of the ancient Greeks – the raising of memorials to the common soldier. It began in the United States after the Civil War, but found particular expression in the years following World War I. The tomb of the Unknown Warrior in Westminster Abbey encloses the corpse of an unidentified British soldier, brought back to England after that war, together with earth from the battlefields of France.

From the sixteenth century onward, many monied people, renowned for nothing but their riches, made bequests for memorial tombs for themselves; less wealthy, but worthy people were commemorated in engraved brass plates; and even the relatively poor saved what money they could to provide for a gravestone. During the nineteenth century this tendency reached its height, with the families and friends of bankers and merchants, even shopkeepers, vying with one another in the magnificence of the monuments over their graves. The cemeteries of Kensal Green in London and Père-Lachaise in Paris are famous for their memorials.

The twentieth century, however, has seen a preference for simplicity. The actor Sir Peter Ustinov has already chosen his epitaph, 'On my grave,' he said, 'I should like them to put: Do not walk on the grass.' He reflected for a moment before adding: 'I wonder whether that shouldn't begin – Please.'

EFFIGIES

The pictorial representation of the deceased goes back many centuries. It began in Egypt, where the portrait statue of Zoser in the Step Pyramid is the oldest known example. The huge memorial statues of Greek kings, the portrait busts of Romans, and the later monuments to popes and kings have already been mentioned (see page 83), but these were essentially formalized, and not necessarily representational.

A more domestic note is struck in Etruscan mortuary art, where the deceased may be shown reclining, sometimes with his wife, on the cover of the casket. (A charming later example of this style is the fifteenth-century tomb at Lowick, in Northamptonshire, of Ralph Green and his wife, which shows the couple holding hands.) During the Roman occupation of Egypt in the early centuries AD, some of the mummy-cases of the local families were painted with actual likenesses.

In medieval France and England, death masks were taken from the bodies of kings and queens, and used for wooden effigies that were placed on top of the coffin while the corpse lay in state. In England, they were later displayed

LEFT: The earliest known effigy of an English king is that of Edward III in Westminster Abbey, London. Taken from a death mask, it reveals, on the left side of his face, signs of the stroke from which he died.

in Westminster Abbey. The earliest known is that of Edward III (died 1377) which clearly shows the distortion of his face due to the stroke that killed him.

It seems that only English examples of these early death masks survive; those in France were destroyed at the time of the Revolution in 1789. The finest is said to be that of Henry VII (died 1509). Later effigies, such as those of William

BELOW: An extended family of the dead is represented at this grave site in Indonesia.

RIGHT: *The stuffed body of Jeremy Bentham, prepared at his behest, and kept in the Senior Common Room of University College, London. His face is a wax model, and the real head is stored at his feet.*

FAR RIGHT: *In 1891, the Parisian surgeon Dr Varlot invented a way of electroplating a dead body with a thin coating of copper.*

FACING PAGE: *In 1780, the bones of more than 20,000 Parisian citizens were removed from Les Innocents Cemetery, and stacked in a labyrinth of underground quarries. They were later joined by millions more. This photograph by the pioneer French photographer Felix Nadar was one of the first taken using artificial light.*

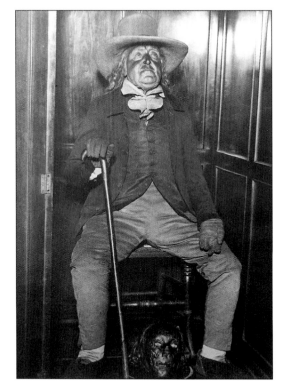

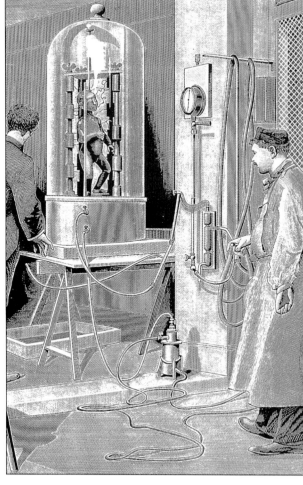

III (died 1702) and his queen Mary (died 1694), were made of wax. When the second Duke of Buckingham died in 1735 while on a tour of Europe, his corpse was preserved, and a replica was made with wax, leather and wood. It is now also in Westminster Abbey.

The strangest effigy of all, however, is that of the English reformer Jeremy Bentham, who died in 1832. He asked for his body to be publicly dissected by Dr Southwood Smith. The skeleton was then to be wired together again, dressed in his clothes, and placed in a glass cabinet to form his 'auto-icon', as he named it. His head was to be embalmed – and he carried a pair of glass eyes ready in his pocket for twenty years – but unfortunately this was not a great success. A wax head was therefore made, and to this day the effigy sits in its cabinet in the Senior Common Room of University College, London, while the real head is kept in a box at its feet.

An even more realistic effigy was made possible by Dr Varlot, a Parisian surgeon in 1891. He used a corpse as one electrode of an electroplating bath. Once immersed in a solution of copper sulphate, the corpse became covered in a deposit of copper one millimetre thick, thus exactly preserving its shape.

CROWDED CEMETERIES

Over the centuries, European burial grounds became crowded places. The growth in population, and the resulting increase in the size of towns and cities, made the problem ever more acute. Coupled with this was the developing realization, by medical men, that local cemeteries, packed with decaying bodies, were a serious threat to health.

In 1763, the authorities in Paris issued a decree that all the church cemeteries in the city were to be closed, and eight municipal cemeteries established on the outskirts. The clergy objected strongly, however, and the decree was not put into practice for many years. Finally, one of the largest cemeteries, Les Innocents, was closed by order in 1780, and the skeletons of more than 20,000 bodies were exhumed and taken to a labyrinth of underground tunnels south of the city, where building stone had previously

RIGHT: A scene from Forest Lawns in California, one of Dr Hubert Easton's 'theme' cemeteries and a far cry from the crowded cemeteries of eighteenth- and nineteenth-century Europe.

been quarried. In due course, these bones were laid out in tidy rows, and the 'catacombs' were opened to public view; eventually they were joined by several million more from other closed cemeteries in the city.

In England, burials exclusively in church cemeteries continued into the 1830s, when the lack of space at last made municipal cemeteries essential. The first was Highgate Cemetery in north London, which was opened in 1839, with an area of seven hectares (17 acres), two of which were unconsecrated, and given over to dissenters and agnostics. Some 170,000 people have been buried there.

BELOW: Highgate Cemetery, in north London, was opened in 1839. Many eminent people have been buried there, including (perhaps most notably) Karl Marx.

The largest cemetery in Britain, in terms of area, is Brookwood Necropolis, in Surrey. It covers 200 hectares (500 acres), and was opened in 1854. At one time, it had its own private railway (charging single fares only for coffins), with a station in London and two at Brookwood – one for Anglicans and the other for Catholics, Jews, and dissenters. Around a quarter of a million bodies are interred there. The most populated cemetery in Europe is also in Britain; this is the City of London Cemetery

at Wanstead, on the east side of London. Half a million bodies are buried there, many of them exhumed from churchyards in the city during the nineteenth century.

In the United States, there are five 'Forest Lawns' in California, the largest of which is in Glendale near Los Angeles. These were the concept of Dr Hubert Easton, who envisaged 'a great park, devoid of misshapen monuments and other signs of earthly death, but filled with towering trees, sweeping lawns, splashing fountains, beautiful statuary and memorial architecture'. Dr Easton's dream is realized in (among many others) the world's largest painting of the Crucifixion, some 60 metres (197 feet) long and 13 metres (43 feet) high, and a stained-glass depiction of the Last Supper, nearly 10 metres (33 feet) long and over 4 metres (13 feet) in height, all of which decorate this modern 'theme' cemetery.

The Russian Piskrevskoe Cemetery in Leningrad covers only 26 hectares (64 acres), but contains the graves of over 470,000 victims of the German siege of Leningrad, which took place between 1941 and 1944. The largest cemetery

in the world is the Rookwood Necropolis in western Sydney, New South Wales. Covering 283 hectares (699 acres), it contains over 600,000 bodies and 200,000 cremated remains.

At Shenhu, in eastern China, some 60,000 graves have been excavated since 1988, in order to reclaim farmland; the bodies are cremated, and stored in a seven-storey crypt. The Memorial Necropole Ecumenica, near San Paolo in Brazil, is ten storeys high, and a similar building has been constructed in Genoa, Italy.

EPITAPHS

When we come across a place of burial, we like to know who is buried there. The earliest inscriptions on tombs and coffins that have survived, and can be translated, are those of the ancient Egyptians. Like the Romans after them, the Egyptians provided little more than brief biographical details of the dead person, with perhaps an invocation to the gods to ensure kind treatment in the afterlife, and a denunciation of anyone who should violate the tomb.

One of the earliest Roman memorial inscriptions found in the British Isles, for example, comes from South Shields in Northumbria:

To the Gods of the lower regions: Regina, freedwoman and wife of Barates of Palmyra, a Catuvellaunian by tribe.

Even more down-to-earth is the runic record on a group of stones set up in Sweden in the 1020s, in memory of Ulv of Borresta:

… and Ulv took three gelds in England.
That was the first that Toste paid.
Then Thorkel paid.
Then Cnut paid.

Some Roman sarcophagi bear the mysterious letters: NF.F.NS.NC. These are an abbreviation for *Non fui – fui – non sum – non curo*, which may be loosely translated as 'I was not – I was – I am

A military honour guard marches through Piskrevskoe Cemetery in Leningrad in 1994, in a ceremony to celebrate the fiftieth aniversary of the lifting of the German siege of the city. The cemetery contains some half-million civilian victims of the siege.

89

The headstone and epitaph of William Bradford, who died in 1752, in the graveyard of Trinity Church, New York. This is the oldest cemetery in the city.

no more – I don't care'. (Compare this with a nineteenth-century inscription from the state of Mississippi: 'Once I Wasn't. Then I was. Now I ain't Again.')

The poet Virgil (70–19 BC), more rhythmically, composed his own epitaph:

Mantua me genuit, Calabri rapuere, tenet nunc Parthenope: Cecini pascua, rura, duces.

('Mantua bore me, Calabria carried me away, now Naples holds me: I sang of meadows, fields, great men.')

The word

'epitaph' comes from the Greek, and means simply 'on a tomb'. But the ancient Greeks made their inscriptions something more, literary and often epigrammatic. The dead heroes of the battle of Thermopylae between the Spartans and the Persians (480 BC) were celebrated by a series of epitaphs attributed to Simonides of Ceos (*c.*556-469 BC), the most famous of which has been translated as:

Go tell the Spartans, thou that passest by,
That here, obedient to their laws, we lie.

For many centuries in Europe, memorial inscriptions – usually in Latin – remained purely factual, but a spark of the Greek wit is to be found in the epitaph of the Netherlands grammarian Jan van Pauteren (1460–1520):

Grammaticam scivit, multos docuitque per annos; Declinare tamen no potuit tumulum.

('Grammar he knew, and taught it many years; however, he could not decline the tomb.')

The brief epitaph composed by the Roman poet Martial (AD 40–104) – *Sit tibi terra levis* ('May the earth lie light upon thee') – found its way later on to many tombstones. Englishman Abel Evans (1679–1737) echoed it satirically in his epitaph for the architect of many great houses, Sir John Vanbrugh, who died in 1726:

Lie heavy on him, earth, for he
Laid many a heavy load on thee.

It was not until the late Middle Ages that the local language had begun to replace Latin in memorial inscriptions. However, as late as 1776, the writer Samuel Johnson (1709–84), asked to write an epitaph in English for the memorial of playwright Oliver Goldsmith, who died in 1774, to be placed in Westminster Abbey, replied that he would not so disgrace the Abbey's walls, and composed it in Latin – for which he was taken to task by many of his friends and colleagues.

The French poet Jean Passerat (1534–1602) took care that his epitaph should be his own. In translation, it reads:

Since now I must fall into the grave,
I, who have always loved peace and rest,
That nothing may weigh heavy
on my ash and bones,
Friends, do not write bad verse upon my
tomb.

Here lies the Body of Mr. WILLIAM BRADFORD Printer, who departed this Life May 23, 1752, aged 92 Years: He was born in Leicestershire, in Old England, in 1660: and came over to America in 1682, before the City of Philadelphia was laid out: He was Printer to this Government for upwards of 50 Years and being quite worn out with Old age and labour, he left this mortal State in the lively Hopes of a blessed Immortality.

Reader, reflect how soon you'll quit this Stage, You'll find but few atain to such an Age. Life's full of Pain. Lo here's a Place of Rest, Prepare to meet your GOD then you are blest.

Here also lies the Body of Elizabeth Wife to the said William Bradford who departed this Life July 8, 1731 aged 68 Years.

RESTORED WITH THE ORIGINAL INSCRIPTION BY THE VESTRY OF TRINITY CHURCH MAY 1863

A direr warning appears on William Shakespeare's tomb – although it was probably not written by the poet himself:

Good friend, for Jesus sake forbeare
To digg the dust enclosed heare;
Blest be the man that spares thes stones
And curst be he that moves my bones.

And a similar, but simpler, plea is to be found on the grave of George Warrington, buried in 1727 in Cornwall:

'Tis my request
My bones may rest
Within this chest
Without molest.

In 1791, John Bowden of Chester published a book entitled: *The Epitaph-Writer; consisting of six hundred original epitaphs, moral, admonitory, humorous and satirical… chiefly designed for those who wish to write or engrave inscriptions on tombstones.*

There is room here to reproduce only one:

Here lies a lewd Fellow, who, while he
drew Breath,
In the Midst of his Life was in Quest of his
Death;
Which he quickly obtain'd for it cost him
his Life,
For being in Bed with another Man's Wife.

Most serious epitaphs, while extolling the virtues of those they commemorate, are otherwise banal. Simpler inscriptions, written with sincerity and feeling, can sometimes be both moving and comic at the same time, as in this from Gloucestershire:

Here lie two babbies, dead as nits,
Who died in agonising fitts;
They were too good to live with we,
So God did take to live with He.

Scotland is rich in epitaphs of this kind. Two from Aberdeen are especially well-known:

Here lie I, Martin Elginbrod,
Have mercy on my soul, Lord God.
As I on you, were I Lord God
And you were Martin Elginbrod.

and

Here lie the bones of Elizabeth Charlotte,
Born a virgin, died a harlot.
She was aye a virgin at seventeen,
A remarkable thing in Aberdeen.

Sometimes, the comic effect can be the result of an accident of grammar:

Erected to the memory of
John MacFarlane
Drowned in the Water of Leith
By a few affectionate friends.

And, perhaps the most famous of all:

Sacred to the memory of
Captain Anthony Wedgwood
Accidentally shot by his gamekeeper
Whilst out shooting.
Well done thou good and faithful servant.

From the eighteenth century onward, many epitaphs made punning reference to the profession of the deceased. The one that Benjamin Franklin wrote for himself is typical:

The body of B. Franklin,
Printer,
Like the cover of an old book
its contents torn out,
and stripped of its lettering and gilding,
lies here, food for worms,
But the work shall not be wholly lost,
for it will, as he believed, appear once
more,
in a new and more perfect edition,
corrected and amended
by the Author.

On the tombstone of a brewer in Liverpool are engraved the words:

Poor John Scott lies buried here,
Though once he was hale and stout.
Death stretched him on his bitter bier,
In another world he hops about.

The grave of Benjamin Franklin in Philadephia is not inscribed with the epitaph he wrote for himself.

91

...R·SI·MONUMENTUM·REQUIRIS·CIRCUMSPICE...

Set into the marble floor of the nave of St Paul's Cathedral in London is the simple memorial inscription to Sir Christopher Wren: 'If you want a monument, look about you'. He rebuilt the cathedral, destroyed in the Great Fire of London in 1666, between 1675 and 1711.

The headstone of Thomas Campbell, a travelling salesman of Chicago who died in 1862, is even more concise:

My Trip is Ended.
Send My samples Home.

Isaac Pitman, the inventor of the shorthand system that is used to this day, was an enthusiast for spelling reform. The memorial to his wife in Lansdown cemetery, Bath, reads:

In memori ov
Meri Pitman
Weif ov Mr Eizak Pitman
Fonetic printer ov this Siti
Deid 19 Agust 1857 edged 64.
'Preper ta mit thei God'

Some epitaphs have included a protest on the part of the surviving relatives against the treatment received by the deceased. A headstone

in Pennsylvania reads, for example:

RANSOM BEARDSLEY
Died Jan 24 1850
Aged 56 years 7 months 21 days
A volunteer in the war of 1812
No pension

And the epitaph of Jonathan Tute, who was buried in Vernon, Vermont, in 1763, includes the verse:

But tho' His Spirits fled on high
his body mould'ring here must lie.
Behold the amazing alteration
Effected by Inoculation
The means Employed his Life to save
Hurried Him Headlong to the Grave.

The epitaph of 26-year-old Ellen Shannon, buried in Girard, Pennsylvania, is even more precise:

*Who was fatally burned
March 21st 1870
by the explosion of a lamp
filled with 'R.E. Danforth's
Non Explosive
Burning Fluid'*

In the early nineteenth century, body-snatching was a constant problem. When Ruth Sprague died in Hoosick Falls, New York State, in 1816, a local medical student secretly exhumed the body for dissection. Her distressed relatives recovered her remains, and raised a stone over her grave:

*She was stolen from the grave
by Roderick R. Clow & dissected
at Dr P.M. Armstrong's office
in Hoosick, NY from which place
her mutilated remains were
obtained and deposited here.
Her body dissected by Fiendish Men
Her bones anatomized,
her soul we trust has risen to God
Where few Physicians rise.*

Many pages could be filled with epitaphs, pithily brief and excessively long, pathetic, flattering, ironic or comic – but, as the tombstone of Joshua Pigg in Norfolk rightly points out:

*Verses on tombs are praises idly spent
A man's good name is his best monument.*

And so, to conclude, here is the epitaph composed by John Cam Hobhouse (1786-1869) for the grave of the best friend of Lord Byron:

*Beneath this stone are deposited the
remains of one who possessed
Beauty without Vanity, Strength without
Insolence, Courage without
Ferocity, and all the Virtues of Man
without his Vices. This praise
which would be unmeaning Flattery, if
inscribed over human ashes,
is but a just Tribute to the Memory of
BOATSWAIN, a dog.*

REMEMBRANCE OF THE DEAD

The epitaph has two functions. On the one hand, it can serve as a brief record of the life of the buried person; but it is also intended to remind us of the previous existence of that person and, in many cases, to ask us to keep that memory alive. One of the most distinguished is that of Sir Christopher Wren in St Paul's Cathedral, which he rebuilt (between 1675 and 1711):

Originally an expression of public sorrow for the deaths of millions of soldiers in World War I, November 11 is also a day for the remembrance of those who died during World War II.

Si monumentum requiris circumspice
(If you want a monument, look about you.)

Many ancient cultures marked the anniversary of a person's death with a feast. More recently this has tended to be a low-key, family affair – if it is celebrated at all – and the occasion merely of a visit to the grave, or a personal expression of sorrow in memory of the departed.

There are exceptions. In England, for example, the events of the English Civil War are still remembered by a small number of people at the statue of Oliver Cromwell (1599–1658) in London, and by a similar commemoration of King Charles I, who was executed, at Cromwell's instigation, in 1649. In Germany, the grave of Johann Wolfgang von Goethe (1749–1832), among others, is similarly honoured; and in France the grave of the rock musician Jim Morrison (1943–71) in Père-Lachaise Cemetery, in Paris, is frequently the scene of hysterical demonstrations by his present-day fans.

The greatest international ceremony in memory of the dead occurs on 11 November each year, when the deaths of millions of soldiers in World War I are solemnly celebrated in Britain, France, Belgium and the United States – and in a notably subdued way in Germany. The loss of so many young men in that war – which, although in a lesser way, was to have an effect on the population of Europe similar to that of the Black Death – had to be marked by an expression of public sorrow, and it is now coupled with remembrance of those who died during World War II.

At a much earlier date, another occasion for the remembering of the dead had been appointed by the Roman Catholic church, at the instigation of Odilo, abbot of Cluny (died 1048). This is All Souls' Day, which is officially on 2 November (or on 3 November if 2 November is a Sunday). Following the celebration of the festival of All Saints on 1 November – dedicated to the memory of all those believed to be in Heaven – this was intended to commemorate those who were thought to be still confined to Purgatory.

In many countries, however, the two ceremonies have become confused. In France, the last days of October see the shops filled with flowering chrysanthemums in pots; these are to be placed around the graves of lost ones on the first day of November. In Mexico, the 'day of the dead' is also 1 November. In a reflection of more primitive rituals, the dead are welcomed back temporarily to the land of the living with gifts of new clothes, drinks and food. They may be enticed to the homes of their relatives by trails of marigolds, or there may be a feast, with music and dancing, at the graveside. Children are given skulls of marzipan or chocolate to eat, and skeletal figures of all kinds can be seen in the streets. In this way, the world of the dead is seen to be intimately mingled with the world of the living.

FACING PAGE: In 1989, nearly 100,000 people attended a candle-lit vigil in Hong Kong, in memory of those who died in Tiananmen Square.

LEFT: Jim Morrison's grave in Paris has become a place of pilgrimage for hundreds of present-day rock fans.

BELOW: On the Day of the Dead in Mexico, children are given skulls of marzipan or chocolate to eat. A reflection of more primitive rituals, this day welcomes the temporary return of the dead to the world of the living.

eus in adiutorium meum intende.
Die ad adiuuandum me festina.
Gloria patri et filio et spiritui sco.
Sicut erat et c. hympne.

CHAPTER 6

LIFE AFTER DEATH

Few people can bear the thought that death could mean the instant and total extinction of every part of themselves. Even if the physical body is finished, surely the gathered experience of a lifetime of work, of creative activity, of educating and caring for others, is not suddenly to be snuffed out like a candle? If there is nothing, absolutely nothing, left after the body has been converted into simple chemicals, is there any point in living at all?

Even from a basic anthropological point of view, there is evidence that this is not entirely the case. We speak, with justification, of the evolution of the human race. If there were not some inherent force driving us forward – the British biologist Richard Dawkins (1941–) called it the 'selfish gene' – there seems no reason why humankind should not have remained at the stage of *Homo pithecanthropus* in which it was little more than just another animal, surviving through the millions of years unchanged, like the crocodile or the cockroach.

Each human generation contributes to the one that follows. As the centuries have passed, we have learnt more about ourselves and the cosmos in which we live. The more progressive communities have learnt how to cure disease and prolong life; they have invented intricate means of transport and communication; they have discovered how to exploit natural resources, and built huge structures; and they have developed art, music, literature and philosophy to a highly sophisticated level.

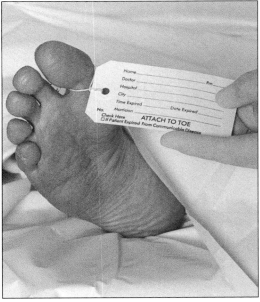

LEFT: Is a dead person no more than a body in the mortuary, so anonymous that a tag on the toe is needed to identify it? Or does something other survive?

Of course, there remain many parts of the world that are devastatingly poor, but even there people wear clothes, have built themselves some kind of shelter, and eat prepared food. And, even in these deprived areas, men and women have emerged as leaders, thinkers, artists, of worldwide standing. They serve, at least, as examples to their own people that improvement is possible.

But, for most human beings, the idea of being little more than fodder to the development of a succeeding generation is not enough. They desperately desire some part of themselves, some justification for the hard work they have put into living, to survive. Otherwise, 'what is it all for?' Out of this desire, maybe, grew the earliest concepts of immortality.

FACING PAGE: The physical resurrection of the dead from their graves. An illustration from the **Book of Hours** *illuminated for the Duc de Berry by the Limburg brothers in the fifteenth century.*

*In the **Inferno** Dante describes how he was led down through the circles of Hell by the Roman poet Virgil. In the eighth circle he found lost souls whose punishment was to have their heads turned backwards on their shoulders. These were those who had dared to foretell the future.*

The living cell is, in a sense, immortal. It can replicate, producing a copy of itself (sometimes, indeed, an improved version, and that is what evolution, in its most fundamental form, is all about). Bacteria and other unicellular organisms can go on reproducing for ever, provided that the conditions in which it lives remain suitable. The pattern of a plant's growth, locked up in the nucleus of its seed, or some other reproductive form, ensures a similar form of immortality. In higher forms of living organisms, the ovum and the sperm carry the message of life everlasting.

But is there something else? Reference was made in Chapter 1 to a 'principle of life'. Although some modern biologists would prefer to deny it, there seems to be something more than mere chemical content in a living organism. And there is another something, even more intangible. We human beings are aware of our existence, and of our individual personalities ahd characters. Most people even feel that other animals have some degree of this awareness as well, although probably not as highly developed as our own. Is this sense of selfhood, perhaps, a manifestation of the principle of life? And should we call it 'the soul'?

THE IMMORTAL SOUL

The concept of the soul – some kind of spiritual element that is distinct from the tangible body – is very old. It occurs even among the most primitive beliefs. The soul is generally regarded as an invisible substance that can be separated from the physical body, and is responsible for those phenomena that distinguish the living from the dead. And, according to some beliefs, sickness and unconsciousness are due to the temporary absence of the soul from the body. Indeed, the Koran states that Allah takes back the soul, not only at death, but every night during sleep, returning it again at wakening.

Human experience of dreams and 'out-of-the-body' phenomena (see page 129) has provided circumstantial evidence that the consciousness is free to roam through time and space, while the body remains in one place. Since consciousness is an essential element of a human body that is truly alive, it was an easy step to identify it with the soul.

Although the soul is usually considered to be invisible, it is not necessarily completely immaterial. Certain beliefs have compared – and in some cases identified – it with a person's

breath or their shadow. And out of this grew the idea of the 'lost soul', an entity separated from the dead or dying body, which might even manifest itself visibly as a ghost (see page 143).

In many relatively primitive beliefs, it is difficult to distinguish the idea of souls from that of ghosts. For instance, the Gonds, an aboriginal tribe of central India, believe that a child in the womb is lifeless until the life-substance, *jiv*, is put into it by Bhagavan, the supreme deity. At death, the *jiv* returns to Bhagavan, but the personality of the dead person remains as the *sanal*.

This *sanal* is believed to linger near the dead body, and it follows the funeral procession to the burial or cremation ground. After the funeral rites, the mourners go to a nearby stream, and place there a small seat, a twig for cleaning teeth, and a cup of water. They order the *sanal* to sit on the seat and rinse his mouth, to purify himself from the pollution of death. Then they sacrifice a fowl or a goat, and cook it, offering the meat to the *sanal*. Later, the *sanal* will visit the house of his surviving kinfolk, and join them in their feasts.

This view of the departed soul – reflected in other funerary rites around the world – is similar to the beliefs of the ancient Greeks. They feared death so much, it seems, that they preferred not to name it and spoke instead in euphemisms: the shade of the 'departed' went to the 'house of Hades'. Hades was the son of the original Titans, and brother of Zeus and Poseidon, and his realm was a dismal place. In the *Odyssey* the shade of Achilles remarks that he would sooner be alive, and the slave of a landless peasant, than king of all the dead.

At the same time, the Greeks developed the concept of the *psyche*, the immaterial aspect of the human soul. In myth, Psyche is represented as an earthly maiden, whose beauty overwhelms Eros, the god of love. He persuades Zeus to raise her to the level of the gods, and make her immortal. In Plato's philosophy this myth illustrates the thesis that love, in its highest form,

IN MANY RELATIVELY PRIMITIVE BELIEFS, IT IS DIFFICULT TO DISTINGUISH THE IDEA OF SOULS FROM THAT OF GHOSTS

is an essential agent of the soul's development.

The ancient Egyptians had a more complicated view of human nature. They thought that the individual was made up of a number of separate constituents. There was the *ka*, a sort of double of the body, a vital force essential to the body's existence. 'To go to one's *ka*' was a euphemism for death. Those who believed that the dead lived on in the tomb had a *ka* statue erected there. Then there was the *ba*, which – though it was closer to the concept of the soul – was rather an independent entity that became

The love of Eros for Psyche, as portrayed by the Italian sculptor Antonio Canova (1757–1822). In Greek philosophy, Psyche represented the immaterial aspect of the human soul, and Plato regarded love as an agent of the soul's development.

*The **ba** – a constituent of the body that was close in concept to that of the soul – was represented by the ancient Egyptians as a bird with a human head.*

separated from the body at death, but remained close by. It was represented as a bird with a human head.

Another important constituent was the heart, but it was seen as something more than the physical organ. It was sometimes known as 'god in man', and was thought of as a recorder of the individual's conduct during life. With all these elements to be considered, an upper-class Egyptian who could afford them put great emphasis on the rites that would follow his or her death. If these rites were performed correctly, the dead person was transformed into an *akh*, or glorified soul.

In the Hindu religion, the soul is known as *atman*. But strict definitions of its nature vary greatly in the scriptural writings, and

> THE HEART…SOMETIMES KNOWN AS 'GOD IN MAN'…WAS THOUGHT OF AS A RECORDER OF THE INDIVIDUAL'S CONDUCT DURING LIFE

among different schools of belief. In its earliest meaning, *atman* was 'breath', a central life-force, and this is the origin of those practices in modern Yoga that involve the control of breathing (see Chapter 1).

The *Upanishads*, the Sanskrit writings that first defined Hindu philosophy some 2,500 years ago, equate *atman* with Brahman, the eternal essence of the whole cosmos. (Even to this day, the Hindu religion recognizes a pantheon of gods, but these are properly regarded as no more than various different aspects of Brahman.) In this view, the selfhood of the individual is something that is experienced, but is incapable of definition. 'This Self – what can you say of it but "no, no!" It is impalpable, for it cannot be grasped; indestructible, for it cannot be destroyed; free from attachment, for it is not attached to anything, not bound. It does not quaver, nor can it be hurt.'

The individual soul, then, is just one part of the all-pervading Brahman (see Chapter 2). Some commentators have likened the totality of existence to a wheel – Brahman is both the hub and the rim, while individual selves are the spokes that connect the two.

Unlike most other religions, however, the Hindu faith does not suppose a single earthly existence, after which the soul is reunited for ever with Brahman. Hindus regard life as being constantly recycled. During each life, an individual's actions can result in a gain or loss of karma. Karma – a Sanskrit word originally meaning 'action' or 'work' – is 'the moral law of cause and effect, by which the sum of a person's actions is carried forward from one life to the next, leading to an improvement or deterioration in that person's fate' (see page 124).

But there is a difficulty here, because there is no definition of the degree of karma that an individual must accumulate, before he or she will be relieved of the burden of further earthly existence. The great Indian classic, the *Bhagavad Gita*, provides some consolation. This work identifies the supreme god as Vishnu-Krishna, 'the base supporting Brahman – immortal Brahman which knows no change – supporting, too, the eternal law of righteousness and absolute beatitude'. Recognizing his own immortality, the individual becomes Brahman:

Once a man has become Brahman, with self serene he neither grieves nor desires… By love and loyalty to me [Krishna] he comes to know me as I really am, how great I am, and who; and once he knows me as I am, he enters me forthwith.

So the *Bhagavad Gita*, like the writings of Plato and many Christian texts, introduced the dual concept of the love of God for man, and the love of man for God. However, the ultimate destination of the individual soul after death is still not defined.

Gautama, the Buddha ('enlightened one') who emerged in India in the sixth century BC, claimed to have found the answer. We live in a world of suffering, to which we constantly return, and from which there is apparently no escape. The cause of suffering, Gautama said, is desire, the way to salvation is to eliminate desire.

The Buddha defined a way that led to transcendence of earthly life: he called it the 'noble eightfold path'. It involved 'perfect understanding, perfect aspiration, perfect speech, perfect conduct, perfect means of livelihood, perfect endeavour, perfect mindfulness, and perfect contemplation'. By following this path, human beings could break the never-ending chain of karma. It led to a state called Nirvana, 'which means the extinction of desire, and therewith of all becoming, of all coming-to-be and passing away'. The individual who achieved this in life became happily free of all craving and, at death, entered 'a timeless citadel to which all the seeming pleasures and real sufferings that bedevil our life have no access'.

The great Hindu god Vishnu-Krishna. 'By love and loyalty to me [a man] comes to know me as I really am, how great I am, and who; and once he knows me as I am, he enters me forthwith.'

ABOVE: *To achieve Nirvana, Buddhists must follow the 'eight-fold' path. These two figures are from a sculptured frieze representing the stages of enlightenment.*

RIGHT: *The shamans of the Tlingit people, on the northwest Pacific coast of America, employed 'soul catchers' to capture the departing soul of a dying person, in an attempt to return it to the sick body. This one has two sealion's heads carved in ivory, and is decorated with abalone shells.*

Buddhist philosophy, then, seems to evade the question of the existence of an individual soul, although it recognizes the law of karma, and the possible eventual absorption of the self into the infinite. The original theravada Buddhism taught that salvation was possible only for the few who succeeded in treading the eightfold path to Nirvana. The more liberal mahayana Buddhism allows for eventual salvation for everyone, and teaches that one who attains enlightenment can choose not to pass into Nirvana, but instead become a Bodhis-attva, remaining behind in the world to help lesser mortals gain enlightenment.

The early Christian Fathers were faced with a dilemma in their view of the soul. They took it for granted that the body and the soul were separate, but they rejected as heresy the Platonic belief that the soul existed independently, and was

immortal. There were two schools of thought. One, traducianism, adhered closely to St Augustine's doctrine of original sin, and believed that the soul was transmitted from one generation to another through procreation.

The other, creationism, held that God created each new human soul afresh. Exactly what happened to the soul at the moment of death was not clear. Thomas Aquinas maintained that the soul was made for the body, but he declared that it could exist temporarily apart from it, in the period between death and the eventual resurrection (see page 110).

In Islamic belief, there are two words for soul. The independent soul, the equivalent to Plato's psyche, is *nafs*. This is the lower, human, aspect of the soul; it needs to be changed, by improving one's way of life, to become a soul at peace. The higher soul is *ruh*, which can be translated as 'spirit'. The Persian mystic Suhrawardi regarded *ruh* as the source of good and *nafs* as the source of evil, the two being in continual conflict.

Ruh is what gives humankind their spiritual dignity, raising them above the animals, and even above the angels. It is immortal: at death it goes

> IN ISLAMIC BELIEF, THERE ARE TWO WORDS FOR THE SOUL…RUH, THE SOURCE OF GOOD, AND NAFS, THE SOURCE OF EVIL, THE TWO BEING IN CONTINUAL CONFLICT

to heaven for assessment, before returning to the tomb to await the final judgment (see page 111). However, the *ruh* of certain individuals – prophets and martyrs – goes straight to heaven without judgment.

But where, within the body, is the soul to be found? As the life principle, it should be present throughout the whole organism; but, as the self, it ought to be located in the mind. For many centuries, philosophers asked themselves this question.

An early suggestion was that the soul was located in the liver – for no reason, except that this organ appeared to have no other function. Aristotle (384–322 BC) favoured the heart; but his contemporary, the anatomist Herophilus, decided that the soul occupied a small region just above the brain stem – an interesting inspiration, in view of modern definitions of

death (see Chapter 1). Other Greek philosophers agreed that the brain was the most likely site, although they were not as specific as Herophilus.

Many centuries later, the French mathematician and philosopher René Descartes (1596–1650) placed the seat of the soul in the pineal gland, a pea-sized organ on top of the mid-brain. Like the liver,

ABOVE: Escorted by St Paul with a drawn sword, the soul of a man is received by St Peter at the Gate of Heaven.

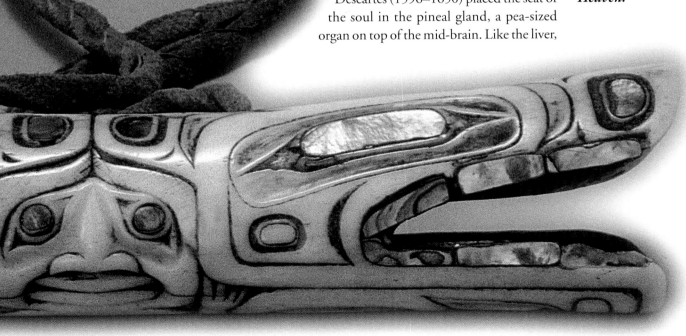

its function was at that time obscure; but it is
now known to process information from the
eyes and limbs. In modern alternative medicine,
it is known as the 'third eye', and is believed to
exert a powerful influence on the workings of
the body.

RESURRECTION

A rather different concept from the immortality
of the soul is that of physical resurrection – the
return to life of the bodies of the dead. In early
religions, resurrection was the prerogative only
of the gods, and was closely linked to the
observation of the cycle of the seasons, with the
apparent death of vegetation at the end of
summer and its rebirth in the spring.

The myths of ancient Egypt, Mesopotamia
and Syria all describe how a god is killed, often
by a wild boar, and his body is thrown into a
river; alternatively, he is drowned. But his death
is mourned by a goddess (sometimes his sister),
and she goes out in search of his corpse; when
she finds him, he returns to life, and his revival
is accompanied by the miraculous recovery of
plant life.

The mourning rituals of the Sumerians for
their god Tammuz were directed to the
preservation of their crops and flocks. They did
not suppose that they could obtain any personal
survival of death: like the ancient Hebrews, they
considered that human immortality was
to be found only in the continuance
of the generations.

One of the first conceptions
of human resurrection is to be
found in Zoroastrianism.
Zoroaster – known in the *Avesta*,
the scriptures of Zoroastrianism,
as Zarathustra – was born at
some time in the seventh
century BC, and declared
himself the prophet of the god
Ahura Mazda, 'the Wise Lord'.
The message of Zoroaster was
that God is One, holy, righteous,
the creator of all things through his
Holy Spirit. The religion is still
practised by a relatively small group who

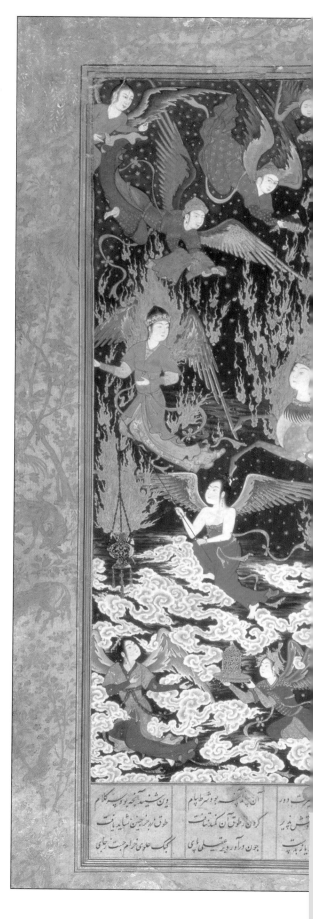

survive in Iran, but also by more than 100,000 Parsees in India (see page 63).

Zoroastrianism was remarkable for its time in that it recognized the possibility of free will, rather than the predestination of the gods: a person could choose to behave well or ill, to follow the way of Ahura Mazda, or of his great adversary Ahriman. The concomitant of this was that the dead had to be judged. At death, the soul had to cross the 'bridge of the requiter'. For the righteous, the bridge was broad, but became 'as narrow as a razor's edge' for the wicked, who as a result fell helplessly into Hell.

Temporarily, the souls remained in the 'House of the Song' (Heaven), or the 'House of the Lie' (Hell), while Ahura Mazda and Ahriman battled for the world. In the end, Ahura Mazda would prevail, the souls would be reunited with their bodies and purged in a sea of molten metal, and all creation would thenceforth enjoy eternal and everlasting bliss.

Despite some confusing aspects of its basic philosophy, Zoroastrianism is essentially a mono-theistic religion, and the idea of judgment and resurrection was developed in the subsequent religions of Judaism, Christianity and Islam.

There is very little reference to resurrection in early Judaic writings. In Jewish literature of the second century BC it was conceived as the physical revival of the dead body, as in the Book of Daniel: 'And many of those who sleep in the dust of the earth shall awake…some to

Young Parsees in an essential initiatory ritual. Parsees are the principal contemporary practitioners of the ancient Zoroastrian religion.

105

everlasting life, and some to shame and everlasting contempt'. Later writings envisaged the renewal of the righteous in a new world, or even their transformation into angels.

Judaism, however, is not a religion of salvation: life on earth is held to be good in itself, and would be worth living without any promise of eternal life to come. The paradox inherent in this view was well expressed by a rabbi of the second century AD:

> *Better one hour of good deeds in this world than the whole life of the world to come – but better one hour of spiritual bliss in the world to come than all the life of this world.*

Original Judaic religious practice was not defined in dogma, and it was left much later to medieval Jewish scholars, above all Moses Maimonides (1135–1204), to lay down the principles of the faith. Maimonides formulated

MEDIEVAL CHRISTIAN SCHOLARS DEVOTED MANY YEARS OF DEBATE TO THE IMPLICATIONS OF RESURRECTION, AND ALTHOUGH POPULAR ICONOGRAPHY CONTINUED TO REPRESENT THE OPENING OF TOMBS, EVEN ORDINARY PEOPLE BEGAN TO QUESTION THE POSSIBILITY OF PHYSICAL RESURRECTION

thirteen principles, which are printed in many Jewish prayer books. The last of these is a declaration of the certainty of resurrection.

At that time, the generally held doctrine was that, when a person died, their soul survived in another place until the resurrection, when it would be reunited with its body on earth. Moses Maimonides, however, advanced the view that resurrection would last for only a short time, and that it is the soul alone that will exist in eternity. Some modern Jewish thinkers believe that this soul is in fact the continuing existence of the entire independent personality, and that this is what is implied in the doctrine of resurrection.

Early Christianity had a very different concept of resurrection. One of the fundamental tenets of the faith, after all, was that Christ had risen from the dead, and Christians expected his imminent return, which would be followed shortly by the end of the old world, and a general physical resurrection along the lines of original Jewish belief.

When this return appeared to be delayed indefinitely, it resulted in a radical restructuring of Christian doctrine. Medieval schoolmen devoted many years of debate to the implications of resurrection: did it really mean that 'the graves would give up their dead', or was it to be regarded rather as a spiritual phenomenon? Although popular iconography continued to represent the opening of tombs, and living persons rising from them, even ordinary people began to question the possibility of physical resurrection. Would they really rise again from the grave in the form in which they were buried – with limbs lost in accidents or war, with bodies decayed from leprosy or cancer?

LEFT: An eighteenth-century imaginary portrait of the Jewish scholar Moses Maimonides.

FACING PAGE: The Christian belief in resurrection was strengthened by the account of the raising of Lazarus from the dead.

107

With the Reformation of the sixteenth century, Christianity developed a number of splinter groups, which have continued to proliferate to the present day. Current orthodox Christianity no longer holds to the belief in physical resurrection, preferring the concept of the eternal existence of the soul, although some creeds still cling to the old ideas.

As for Islam, the Koran is unequivocal about the forthcoming resurrection: 'O ye men! If you are in doubt about the Resurrection, We remind you, so as to convince you, that We created you… Allah is the Truth, because He quickens the dead, because He is almighty, because the end of the world will come, there is no doubt therein, and because Allah will waken those who are in the tombs.'

The judgment of Anhai. Jackal-headed Anubis adjusts the balance, while ibis-headed Thoth records the result of the weighing.

'AS FOR ANY MAN WHO SHALL ENTER INTO THIS TOMB AS HIS MORTUARY POSSESSION, I WILL SEIZE HIM LIKE A WILD FOWL; HE SHALL BE JUDGED FOR IT BY THE GREAT GOD…'

JUDGMENT

Final judgment of the dead – but without any implication of physical resurrection – is a very old concept. The earliest evidence of this belief occurs in ancient Egyptian records from around 2400 BC. It appears to be based on the idea that, in the afterlife, accusations might be brought against the dead, just as they were brought in juridical courts against the living.

This is exemplified in the tomb inscription of Herkhuf, an Aswan noble, which begins with a dire warning to grave robbers:

As for any man who shall enter into this tomb as his mortuary possession, I will seize him like a wild fowl; he shall be judged for

*it by the Great God... I was one saying
good things and repeating what was loved.
Never did I say aught evil to a powerful one
against any person, for I desired that it
might be well with me in the Great God's
presence.*

The idea that the dead would be impartially
judged developed into an image of their good and
bad deeds being weighed in the balance. The
Papyrus of Anhai, now in the British Museum,
in London, represents the scene. The balance is
being adjusted by the jackal-headed god Anubis;
in one pan is Anhai's heart in a mortuary jar, and
in the other the feather symbol of Maat – truth.
To the right stands Thoth, the ibis-headed god
of wisdom, recording the result of the weighing.

The verdict appears in the adjacent text, 'His
ba has stood in witness thereof. His case is exact
on the Great Balance. No crime has been found
in what he has done.' Had Anhai been found
guilty, his fate is clear: below the balance stands
the threatening presence of the monster Am-
mut, 'eater of the dead'.

The Jewish conception of the last judgment
developed at a time when the nation of Israel
was suffering a series of persecutions around the
start of the first century BC, and began to hope
for divine intervention, and the end of the world.
The 'apocalyptic' text known as Esdras states:

*And the earth shall restore those that are
asleep in her, and so shall the dust those that
dwell in silence, and the secret places shall
deliver those souls that are committed unto
them. And the Most High shall be revealed
on the seat of judgment, and compassion
shall pass away, and longsuffering shall be
withdrawn; but judgment only shall
remain...*

*And the pit of torment shall appear, and
over against it shall be the place of rest; and*

ABOVE: **The
entrance to Hell
was frequently
depicted as the
gaping mouth of a
great beast.
According to
medieval Christian
beliefs, Christ
descended to Hell
in the interval
between his
crucifixion and
resurrection, and
there defeated
Death.**

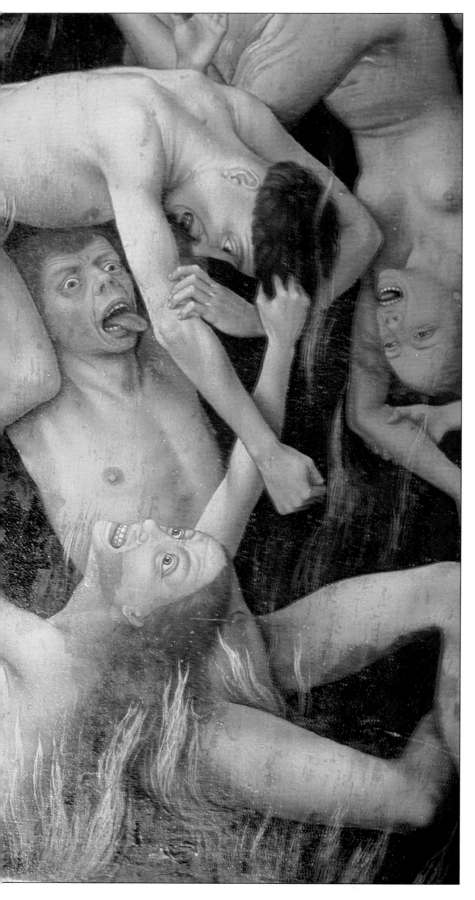

the furnace of hell shall be shewed, and over against it the paradise of delight. And then shall the Most High say to the nations that are raised from the dead, see and understand whom ye have denied, or whom ye have not served, or whose commandment ye have despised. Look on this side and that; here is delight and rest, and there fire and torments. Thus shall he speak unto them in the day of judgment.

This idea greatly influenced early Christian belief, and found its most dramatic expression in the Revelation of John:

Then I saw a great white throne, and Him who sat upon it; from his presence earth and sky fled away, and no place was found for them. And I saw the dead, great and small, standing before the throne, and books were opened. Also another book was opened, which is the Book of Life. And the dead were judged by what was written in the books, by what they had done. And the sea gave up the dead in it, Death and Hades gave up the dead in them, and all were judged by what they had done.

When the imminent return of Christ did not occur, generations of Christians had to come to terms with the realization that they would die before that promised event. The concept then arose of an interim judgment at death, which would be followed eventually by the Last Judgment. From this came the idea of Purgatory: immediately after death, the soul would be judged and sent to Purgatory – unless its sins were so great that it was already damned beyond redemption. Lesser sins were expiated in Purgatory, so that the dead could hope for forgiveness at the Last Judgment, and be admitted to Paradise. Interestingly, many medieval representations of the final judgment show the souls being weighed in the balance, just as in Egyptian papyri of more than 2,000 years before.

At the Last Judgment, the irredeemable sinners are cast down to eternal punishment in Hell. A detail from a painting by the Flemish painter Rogier van der Weyden (1400–64).

LEFT: The concept of the weighing of souls at judgment is found, not only in ancient Egyptian and Islamic belief, but in many medieval Christian representations. This is a twelfth-century sculptured panel from the cathedral of Notre Dame in Paris.

The immediate judgment of the Islamic dead in the tomb has been described in Chapter 4. Those who correctly answer the questioning by Munkar and Nakir are permitted a view of Paradise, while those who cannot answer, and infidels, remain in the grave until the end of the world. The Koran says:

> O ye men, fear your Lord!. The end of the world will be a terrible thing. On the day thou shalt see it, every suckling mother shall forsake the child she suckles, every pregnant woman will miscarry, and men thou shalt see drunken, though they be not drunken, so dreadful shall be the punishment of Allah…
> We have ordained all deeds in every detail, and have fastened on the neck of each man the reckoning of his Destiny. On the resurrection day, We will offer him a Book which he will find wide open.

The statement that everything is recorded in this book implies that it is vain for a man to attempt to defend himself; however, one chapter of the Koran does allow for this possibility. There are also several references to balances, where good and bad deeds are placed in the appropriate scales, men being judged according to which is the heavier.

In the ancient *Vedas* of India, it was the judge of the underworld, King Yama, who determined who had been sincere, and who had lied. Later Indian texts describe, as in other religions, the weighing of good and evil. Chinese Buddhism also has a specific judge of the dead, Yen-lo Wang. In Japanese Buddhism the name of the judge is Emma-O; he has the sinner weighed, and the accused's sins are reflected in a mirror before judgment is passed.

BELOW: A light-hearted view, from eighteenth-century India, of the paths to Heaven and Hell represented as a game of Snakes and Ladders.

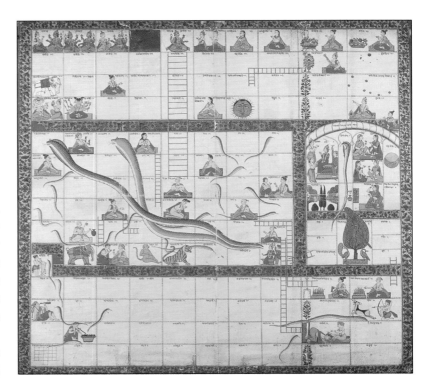

CHAPTER 7

THEIR SPIRITS ARE WITH US

Although anthropologists commonly use the term 'ancestor worship', this practice should not be thought of as elevating the dead to the status of a deity. It derives from the belief that the dead remain close to the living, perhaps for a considerable time; they must be commemorated with honour, provided with whatever they need, placated so that they do not interfere when it is inconvenient, but at the same time asked, as intermediaries with the gods, for help when it is necessary.

ANCESTOR WORSHIP

Essentially this belief is found among close-knit societies, where the sense of kinship is strong, and survived particularly, in its original form, in Africa and Melanesia. Among the Manus of the Bismarck Archipelago in Papua New Guinea, for instance, the spirit of the living male member of a household – known as 'Sir Ghost' – was the 'god' of the family. When he died, he was replaced by his successor, but his skull was placed above the entrance to the house, where it protected the family from malign influences, and rewarded or punished family members according to their deeds. Those who did wrong had their 'soul stuff' removed, and became ill; if the misdeed was serious enough, they died.

The dead of the Trobriand Islanders had two spirits. One was a simple ghost that vanished after a few days; the other, *baloma*, existed as an eternal ancestral spirit in the land of the dead. The *baloma* was venerated,

LEFT: In Papua New Guinea, the skull of an ancestor is solemnly decorated with a ring of feathers.

FACING PAGE: Each year the people of the Trobriand Islands near Papua New Guinea celebrate the spirits of their dead ancestors in the belief that they help in the raising of their crops.

113

RIGHT: In this photograph, taken surreptitiously in 1890 in South Dakota, the Sioux are gathering for a performance of the Ghost Dance.

BELOW: Wearing their 'ghost shirts', the Sioux believed they were protected from bullets. But at Wounded Knee in 1890, the shirts proved powerless against guns, and some 300 men, women and children were massacred.

and was believed to bring help in the raising of crops; every year it returned to its village to join in a feast, and it could also appear to the locals in visions and dreams.

Among the indigenous people of North America, the Pueblo peoples of the southwest practised elaborate ritual celebration of their ancestors. These were impersonated in ceremonies, and asked to bring rain, plentiful crops, and other blessings.

In 1870, a new faith arose among the Paiute of western Nevada. It began with a dreamer named Ta'vibo, and eventually centred around his son Wovoka – known to the whites as 'Jack Wilson'. On 1 January 1889 there was an eclipse of the sun, and, as Wovoka later reported:

> *When the sun died, I went up to heaven and saw God and all the people who died a long time ago. God told me to come back and tell my people that they must be good and love one another, and not fight or steal or lie. He gave me this dance to give to my people.*

Wovoka said that their ancestral lands would be returned to the Indians, and there would be a great reunion between the living and their ancestors. All they had to do was give up alcohol, cease farming and their traditional funeral rites – and regularly perform what came to be known as the 'Ghost Dance'.

This was unlike any other ceremonial dance. The dancers, men and women, linked fingers in a series of circles, one inside the other, and slowly shuffled round anticlockwise to follow the track of the sun. The dance was performed for four or five days running, accompanied by chanting but without any musical instruments.

Reports of Wovoka's message soon spread, and reached the Sioux of the Great Plains in October 1890. Two men named Kicking Bear and Short Bull brought the news to Sitting Bull. The word from Wovoka was that, the following spring, the ground would be covered over with new earth that would bury all the white men. The people who had danced the Ghost Dance would be carried up into the air while the wave of new earth was passing; then they would be set down again among the ghosts of their ancestors.

Kicking Bear had his own addition to make to the new belief. This was the 'ghost shirt', made of cloth or buckskin and painted with magic symbols that would protect its wearer from

bullets. The Sioux also adopted the deliberate use of hypnotic trance, which they believed would put them into direct communication with their ancestors.

By the end of the year, the Ghost Dance was being performed throughout the American West; but, although Wovoka's message was essentially a peaceful one, it alarmed white officials in the reservations. The local agency representative at Standing Rock in the Dakotas, James McLaughlin, ordered the arrest of Sitting Bull. In the early hours of 15 December 1890, the old chief and thirteen of his people were killed in a struggle, and the remainder fled to join Kicking Bear in the Badlands nearby. Pursued by white and Indian troops, they turned to fight at Wounded Knee creek, confident of the protection of their ghost shirts. But the shirts were powerless against four Hotchkiss guns, and some 300 men, women and children were slaughtered indiscriminately.

The Ghost Dance continued for some years in the southwest, particularly among the Kiowa, but the massacre at Wounded Knee finally destroyed all hope of ancestral return.

The best-known form of ancestor worship was that practised in China and Japan, although

ABOVE: **On the festival of Tsing Ming, a day devoted to reverencing dead ancestors, a Chinese woman takes her husband's bones from their funerary jar in a Shanghai cemetery. After cleaning them carefully, she will replace them until the following year.**

LEFT: **Framed pictures of dead relatives form an ancestral shrine in a Chinese street.**

it has declined sharply in the twentieth century. Reverence for old people was an essential part of the teachings of Confucius in the sixth century BC, and the family was regarded as a close-knit group that comprised both the living and the dead. Ancestral shrines were erected in the home, and tablets inscribed with the names of the more recent ancestors, as well as those particularly celebrated, were kept there. Memorial rites were held in front of these tablets, and also at temples and graveyards.

Confucianism became deeply influenced by Buddhism, and it was during the sixth century AD that the Chinese form of Buddhism reached Japan. There it attained a state of co-existence with the earlier Shinto religion. In due course, Shinto became principally concerned with everyday life, while Japanese Buddhism stressed the importance of funeral rites and ceremonies of commemoration.

NECROMANCY

The idea that the dead, by virtue of their existence in a state halfway between the living and the gods, were in a position to know what the future held is both a very primitive and a relatively sophisticated one. On the one hand, the magicians of the earliest societies claimed to be able to conjure up the spirits of the dead to assist them in their predictions; yet the Greeks and the Romans also believed that ghosts could appear to prophesy the future.

'Necromancy' comes from the Greek, and means literally 'divination by the dead'. There is a very detailed description in Lucan's *Pharsalia* of a necromantic operation. Sextus Pompeius (66–35 BC), during his revolution against Rome, wished to discover what fate held in store for him, and decided to consul the witch Erichtho. 'Though it may be well enough for the oracles

THE IDEA OF NECROMANCY WAS THAT THE DEAD, BY VIRTUE OF THEIR EXISTENCE IN A STATE HALFWAY BETWEEN THE LIVING AND THE GODS, WERE IN A POSITION TO KNOW WHAT THE FUTURE HELD

and prophets who serve the Olympians to give riddling responses, a man who dares to consult the dead deserves to be told the truth.'

Erichtho had 'kept on good terms with the infernal powers by squatting in tombs', and had also surrounded herself with flesh and bones from children's funeral pyres, graveclothes, and fragments of buried corpses. To carry out her ritual, she asked for a recent corpse, with sound lungs, because those long dead 'only squeak incoherently'. Erichtho cut open the body, and poured a disgusting mixture of substances into its veins; then she embarked on a long and outlandish incantation, invoking all the ancient gods associated with death.

A ghost materialized, but at first it refused to enter the corpse. Erichtho threatened it with the pains of hell; and slowly the body came to life, and sprang up. It answered all the questions put to it by Pompeius and then, as its reward, was cremated.

Later, necromancy was forbidden by Roman law, and thereafter it was regarded as 'the blackest of the black arts'. The Christian Church declared it a major crime, quoting the fate of Saul, as described in the first book of Samuel, as a dreadful example.

Saul, the first king of Israel, became obsessively jealous of his henchman David, who was compelled to flee into the Negev desert, where he allied himself with the Philistines.

Then Saul said unto his servants, Seek me a woman that hath a familiar spirit, that I may go to her, and enquire of her. And his servants said unto him, Behold, there is a woman that hath a familiar spirit at En-dor.

Saul went to her, and asked her to conjure up the spirit of Samuel.

And Samuel said to Saul, Why hast thou disquieted me, to bring me up? And Saul answered, I am sore distressed; for the

FACING PAGE: Saul, the first king of Israel, visited the witch of En-dor, who summoned up the spirit of Samuel with a dire prophecy.

1. Samuel. Chap. XXVIII. Ver. 15.

APPARITION OF SAMUEL

RIGHT: *Dr John Dee (1527–1608), a mathematician and occultist, was reputed to have performed a necromantic ceremony.*

Philistines make war against me, and God is departed from me, and answereth me no more… therefore I have called thee, that thou mayest make known to me what I shall do. Then said Samuel… The Lord hath rent the kingdom out of thine hand, and given it to thy neighbour, even to David, because thou obeyedest not the voice of the Lord… Moreover, the Lord will also deliver Israel with thee into the hand of the Philistines, and tomorrow shalt thou and thy sons be with me…

Sure enough, three of Saul's sons were killed shortly after in the battle of Gilboa, and Saul, mortally wounded, took his own life. As the *Catholic Encyclopedia* puts it:

The Church does not deny that, with a special permission of God, the souls of the departed may appear to the living, and even manifest things unknown to the latter. But, understood as the art or science of evoking the dead, necromancy is held by theologians to be due to the agency of evil spirits.

Nevertheless, necromancy continued to be practised, occasionally and secretly, until after the Middle Ages. Dr John Dee, the sixteenth-century mathematician and occultist (1527–1608), was reputed to have performed a necromantic ceremony, but this accusation is most likely to be attributed to the common fear of his magical activities. And popular opinion continued to insist that ghosts (see Chapter 6) could appear and give dire warnings of events to come.

RIGHT: *Inspired by the 'spirit rappings' produced by the Fox Sisters, people began to hold sittings in their own homes. Soon, societies formed to investigate the phenomenon further.*

SPIRITUALISM

By the eighteenth century, surviving belief in magic and other occult practices was giving way in western Europe to rationalism, the conviction that everything could be explained by natural causes. Nevertheless, as Samuel Johnson (1709–84) declared:

It is wonderful that five thousand years have elapsed since the creation of the world, and still it is undecided whether or not there has ever been an instance of the spirit of any person appearing after death. All argument is against it, but all belief is for it.

In 1848, a series of strange events took place in the home of the Fox family in Hydesville, a small hamlet in New York State. For three months, John Fox, his wife and their two youngest daughters had been kept awake by strange rapping noises. Mrs Fox described what happened on the night of Friday 31 March 1848. 'The children, who slept in the other bed in the room, heard the rapping, and tried to make similar sounds by snapping their fingers… Then Margaretta said, in sport, "Now do just as I do. Count one, two, three, four," striking one hand against the other at the same time – and the raps came as before. She was afraid to repeat them.

I then thought I could put a test that no one in the place could answer. I asked the

a public demonstration of 'spirit rappings'. It caused a sensation, and they followed it up with performances throughout the eastern United States. Their popularity was undiminished by the suggestion of three eminent professors from Buffalo University, that the sounds were made by the girls' knee-joints, or by the allegation that Kate had confessed to cracking her toes.

The girls' claim to be acting as a medium between the spirit and everyday worlds quickly caused a quasi-scientific interest in 'mediumship' to sweep the western world. People who attended one of their demonstrations, or who had merely heard about them, began to hold sittings themselves – soon dubbed 'seances', from the French – in their own homes. If the results were successful, they joined together and formed societies to investigate the phenomenon further. Persons ('mediums') emerged who were able almost to guarantee positive demonstrations, and gradually the movement gained religious, rather than scientific, significance, so that, by the 1870s, many societies were already calling themselves 'churches'.

The newly named Spiritualism was introduced to Britain in 1852 by an American medium, Mrs Hayden, and in 1865 an Association of Progressive Spiritualists was formed in Darlington, County Durham. Attempts to form a national association were for a long time unsuccessful, but eventually the Spiritualists' National

LEFT: The Fox sisters' reputation was such that fanciful illustrations such as this were commonplace in periodicals of the time, despite the fact that they claimed no powers of levitation, only the ability to provoke 'spirit rappings'.

BELOW: Dramatically lit, a medium enters a trance in an attempt to contact individuals in the spirit world. His audience eagerly await messages from those who have 'passed over'.

'noise' to rap my different children's ages successively. Instantly, each one of my children's ages was given correctly, pausing between them sufficiently long enough to individualize them to the seventh – at which a longer pause was made, and then three more emphatic raps were given, corresponding to the age of the little one that died, which was my youngest child.
I then asked, 'Is this a human being that answers my questions correctly?' There was no rap. I asked, 'Is it a spirit? If it is, make two raps.' Two sounds were given as soon as the request was made.

Now, knowing what investigators have discovered about 'poltergeist' activity (see page 149), these events can be seen as distinctly suspect. It was not true that 'no one in the place could answer' Mrs Fox's questions; apart from John Fox himself, there were the two teenage girls, Margaretta and Kate.

However, news of the 'haunting' spread rapidly, and crowds of sensation-seekers besieged the Foxs' tiny cottage. Mrs Fox took Margaretta and Kate away to stay with a married daughter in Rochester, and there, in 1849, the girls gave

RIGHT: **D.D. Home held a seance in 1868, when he allegedly rose into the air, then floated out of one third-floor window and in at the next.**

FACING PAGE: **In 1874, Sir William Crookes held a series of seances with Florence Cook. She claimed to be able to materialize as 'Katie King', the daughter of the seventeenth-century buccaneer Sir Henry Morgan. This photo was produced as proof.**

BELOW: **Other 'spirit photographs' are far less convincing. This picture of a 'ghost' appearing above a baby's crib is obviously a fake.**

Union Ltd was formed in 1902, and remains the largest organization of its kind in Britain. Although a degree of interest in Spiritualism was taken in many other European countries, Britain and the United States were the principal centres of the movement until the mid-twentieth century.

However, they now have an active rival. Not long after the emergence of the Fox sisters, an offshoot of Spiritualism was developed in France by Dr Hippolyte Leon Denizard Rivail (1804–69). It differed from Spiritualism in that its emphasis was on reincarnation (see page 124), and Dr Rivail adopted the name 'Allan Kardec' on the basis of information he received, in a seance, about his former lives. His book, *The Book of Spirits*, was published in 1856, and a copy was taken to Rio de Janeiro by a Brazilian nobleman. There a new religion, named Spiritism, sprang up, which combined Kardec's Spiritualism with both Christian, and African voodoo, beliefs, and has since spread to other countries, particularly the Philippines. Currently, there are more than 3,000 Spiritist centres in Brazil alone. With its emphasis on healing, the movement has become closely associated with the 'psychic surgeons' who claim to be able to perform operations without the use of anaesthetics, and without leaving any bodily trace.

In Europe and America meanwhile, although 'spirit rappings' remained the foundation of Spiritualism, they soon proved insufficient as phenomena for the growing band of mediums, who looked for more visible manifestations. Table-turning became popular, and some mediums – notably the Scot Daniel Dunglas Home (1833–86) – were alleged to materialize objects, move others without touching, and even achieve levitation. (Quite what this had to do with contacting the spirit world is not clear.)

As the technique of photography became commercially available, a number of people claimed to have obtained photographs of materialized spirits. The first was William Mumler, a Boston jeweller, who experimented with a self-portrait in 1861. When the plate was developed, he detected what he took to be the image of a ghost standing beside him. Numerous photographs of a similar kind were subsequently produced in the course of seances, but most of these are obviously no more than tricks of the light, and some are transparent fakes.

> THE SPIRITIST MOVEMENT HAS BECOME CLOSELY ASSOCIATED WITH 'PSYCHIC SURGEONS' WHO CLAIM TO BE ABLE TO PERFORM OPERATIONS WITHOUT THE USE OF ANAESTHETICS

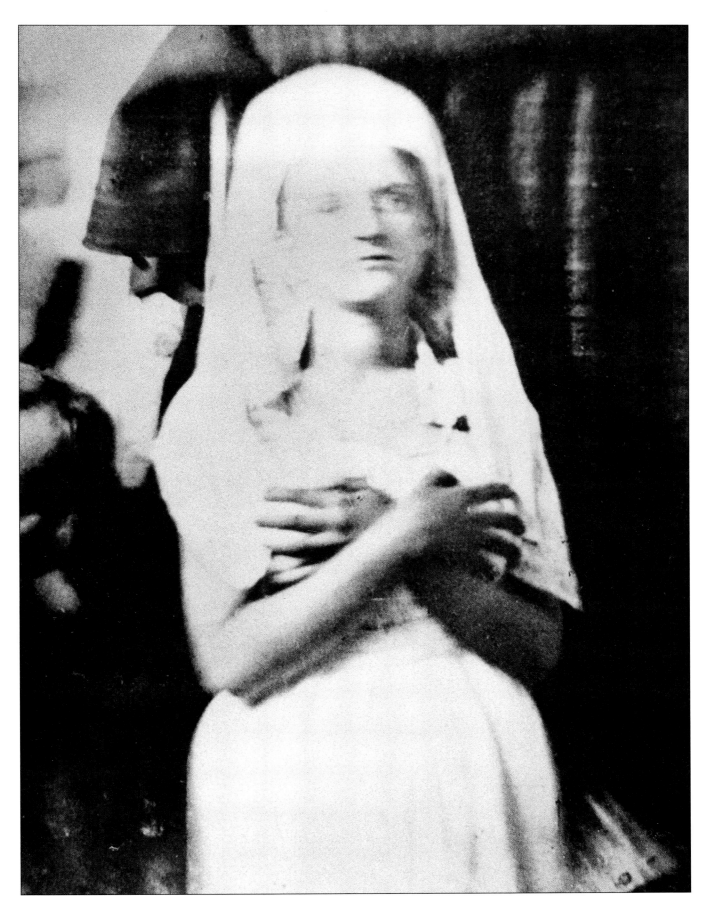

The 'National Laboratory for Psychical Research' was set up by Harry Price, the most notorious investigator of psychical phenomena in England during the 1930s.

One of the characteristic developments among mediums has been their ability to go into trance. Aside from the 'physical' mediums, there are those who then claim to be in direct communication with individuals in the spirit world – their 'spirit guides'. They have produced messages by automatic writing – where the medium goes into a light trance, and writes without being aware what he or she is writing – or spoken in voices that are very different from their own. Some of the results are remarkable, with specific messages for people attending the seance, but there is no evidence to establish that the information has not been obtained by telepathy, rather than from a spirit communicator.

What do Spiritualists believe? It is difficult to generalize, but certain beliefs appear to be common to all. Humankind is composed of two elements, a mortal body and an immortal spirit. At death, the spirit leaves the body, and enters a 'spiritual plane'. There are seven of these planes,

of which earth is the lowest state of existence. The second plane – often referred to as 'Summerland' – is a level of existence that is not unlike that on earth, except that there is no pain or suffering, and there is also the opportunity for further spiritual advancement.

Those who have done evil on earth, or do not display sufficient faith, will find themselves, after physical death, alone in a sort of fog-bound limbo; they have become too attached to material things to be able to leave the earth, and these are those who appear as ghosts. Some Spiritualist societies organize 'rescue circles' to bring such lost souls to repentance.

In America, the National Spiritual Association of Churches was founded in 1893, and in 1899 it adopted a Declaration of Principles. These included:

(1) We believe in Infinite Intelligence. (2) We believe that the phenomena of Nature, both physical and spiritual, are the expres-

sion of Infinite Intelligence. (3) We affirm that a correct understanding of such expression, and living in accordance therewith, constitute true religion. (4) We affirm that the existence and personal identity of the individual continue after the change called death. (5) We affirm that communication with the so-called dead is a fact, scientifically proven by the phenomena of Spiritualism.

THE CROSS-CORRESPONDENCES

One of the most interesting experiments organized by the Society for Psychical Research (SPR – see Chapter 8) is known as the 'cross-correspondences'. A group of members agreed to attempt to send messages, after their deaths, to still-living friends. Because of what subsequently occurred, it is believed that, in order to make the experiment more convincing, they agreed each to send only part of a message; the meaning of the whole would become apparent only when the various parts were put together. The complete report of the experiment is complex, involving as it does many references to classical literature (with which the participants were familiar), and a single example must suffice.

On 16 April 1907, a Mrs Fleming, who was not a professional medium, produced a piece of automatic writing in India. It read, 'Maurice. Morris. Mors. And with that the shadow of death fell upon him and his soul departed out of his limbs' (*mors*, of course, is the Latin for 'death'). On the following day, in England, Leonora Piper (a famous American professional medium, and the only one in the experimenting group) spoke the words, 'Sanatos... Tanatos' as she emerged from trance. *Thanatos* is the Greek for 'death'.

On 29 April, a Mrs Verrall produced a long message in automatic writing. It began with a slightly garbled quotation from the poet Walter Savage Landor – 'warmed both hands before the Fire of Life, it fails, and I am ready to depart' – and was followed by a quotation in Latin from Virgil describing the early death of the nephew of the Roman emperor Augustus. Then came the first four words from Shakespeare's 'Come away, come away, death' and, finally, a long

quotation in Latin from the Roman poet Horace about death.

Taken by itself, this example is not over-convincing; after all, the ladies were already prepared to receive messages from their dead friends. However, in full, the 'cross-correspondences' are difficult to dismiss. What is notable is that, for all their ingenious word-games, the participants – if it was truly their surviving spirits who indulged in them – were unable to confirm the basic beliefs of Spiritualism.

Let the alleged spirit of SPR member F.W.H. Myers have the last word:

The nearest simile I can find to express the difficulties of sending a message – is that I appear to be standing behind a sheet of frosted glass – which blurs sight and deadens sounds – dictating feebly – to a reluctant and somewhat obtuse secretary. A feeling of terrible impotence burdens me – I am powerless to tell what means so much – I cannot get into communication with those who would understand and believe me.

The poet and essayist F.W.H. Myers, one of the leading members of the Society for Psychical Research in its early years.

REINCARNATION

RIGHT: *Pythagoras, the eminent Greek philosopher of the sixth century BC, was a firm believer in the trans-migration of souls. Legend has it that he disappeared for several months, and on his return told acquaintances that he had been in the Underworld. This painting by Salvator Rosa (1615–73) depicts the event.*

Belief in reincarnation – rebirth of the soul after death into a new physical body – is very old. It forms an important part of the religion of some two-thirds of the modern population of the world – not only tribal societies in Africa and Australasia, but Hindus, Buddhists and even some western cults. As the English author Rider Haggard (1856–1925) wrote, 'The Personality which animates each one of us is immeasurably ancient, having been forged in many fires.'

The body to which the soul returns does not have to be human. The ancient Greeks, such as the philosopher Pythagoras (580–500 BC), held that reincarnation could occur in animal form, and the Hindus also believe that an individual who has lost karma during his or her life (see page 101) can return as a lower form of life – a cactus, a lizard, or a toad. Some Australian

RIGHT: *According to Buddhist belief, Bodhisattvas will return voluntarily time after time, and will continue to do so until all human beings are saved.*

Aboriginal tribes believe that the soul can even reincarnate in inanimate things such as rocks.

Early Buddhism denied the existence of a separate personal identity – each of us being only a succession of continually changing physical and mental states – yet it accepted that human beings live many lives. This apparent paradox is explained in the belief that what passes from one life to another is an insubstantial 'something', like a flame from one candle to another.

The length of time between reincarnations can also vary greatly. It may be immediate, many years, or even centuries. Bodhisattvas (see page 102) return voluntarily time after time, and will continue to do so until all human beings are saved. The Tibetans believe that the bodhisattva Avalokitesvara became incarnate as the Dalai Lama, and that each successive Dalai Lama is his reincarnation. When a Dalai Lama dies, his soul immediately occupies the body of a child born at the moment of his death, and a special

declared that she had had a previous existence, and named the place of her former birth. When she was taken there, she correctly pointed out places where she had secretly hidden her toys, and identified her relatives and former husband.

Interest in the possibility of reincarnation has revived in the West, and has recently been coupled with hypnosis. The practice derives from the psychiatric use of 'regression', in which the patient is enouraged to uncover unpleasant past experiences that have been repressed, but which are responsible for the present trauma. 'Hypnotic regression' has revealed some startling examples of what are believed to be past lives. A case that provoked wide public interest was that of 'Bridey Murphy'.

Between November 1952 and October 1953, an American amateur hypnotist named Morey Bernstein, of Pueblo, Colorado, carried out a series of regressions with Mrs Virginia Tighe – whose real identity he concealed under the pseudonym of Ruth Simmons in his book, *The Search for Bridey Murphy* (1956). During the sessions, which were tape-recorded, Mrs Tighe said that she had previously been Bridey Murphy, the daughter of an Irish barrister, and had been born in County Cork on 20 December 1798.

From session to session, the speech of the Colorado housewife – who had been born in

BELOW: The Tibetans believe that the original Dalai Lama, Avalokitesvara, is reincarnated in each of his successors. When a lama dies, a committee must set out to find a child born at the moment of his death, and examine him for signs that he is the true reincarnation.

committee of lamas must set out at once to find and examine the child.

In Chinese Buddhism, the goddess Meng P'o makes all the souls of the dead drink a bitter-sweet brew before they return to another life, so that they will not recollect the deeds of their previous existence. This is very like the belief of the ancient Greeks that the dead drank of the waters of Lethe, the river of forgetfulness.

Nevertheless, there have been 'highly evolved' souls who claim to remember their past lives. The Greek philosopher Empedocles (490–430 BC) is said to have remembered existing as a fish, a bird, a maiden and a youth. The Theosophist Annie Besant (1847–1933) believed she had been (among other incarnations) the female martyr Hypatia (died AD 415) and the philosopher Giordano Bruno (1548–1600) who was burnt at the stake in Rome.

In 1926, an Indian girl named Shanti Devi was born in Delhi. During her childhood, she

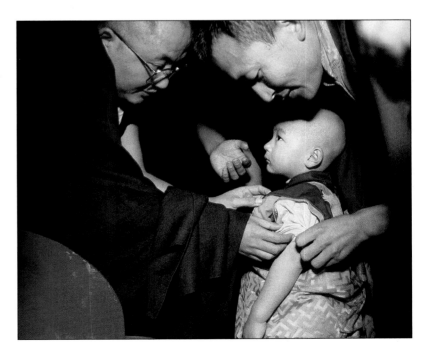

RIGHT: Arnall Bloxham (right), the hypnotherapist who 'regressed' some of his subjects into their apparent past lives. Recently doubt has been cast on many of his cases, and it is suggested that subjects had unconsciously remembered salient incidents from books, films or television broadcasts.

BELOW: The book, first published in 1956, which recorded Mrs Virginia Tighe's 'memories' as Bridey Murphy, caused a furore in the press.

Wisconsin, and lived in Chicago until her marriage – took on a stronger Irish accent, and became more personal. She gave details of her childhood, and described how, though herself a Protestant, she had married a Catholic, Sean Brian Joseph MacCarthy, at the age of 20. The couple had travelled to Belfast, where a second marriage ceremony was performed at St Theresa's, the church of Father John Gorman.

Bernstein's book, which was subsequently made into a film, attracted a great deal of press criticism. *The Chicago Daily News* serialized it, and the *Chicago American* immediately attacked it, claiming (without confirmatory evidence) that Mrs Tighe had got her information from an Irish-born aunt. William Barker, a journalist from the *Denver Post*, spent three weeks in Ireland, trying to track down details from Mrs Tighe's story. Some – such as the names of shops she claimed to have dealt with in Belfast – proved to be correct, but Barker ran up against an insuperable stumbling-block: births, marriages and deaths had not been recorded in Ireland until 1864, the year 'Bridey Murphy' died. And he could find

no trace of St Theresa's, or Father Gorman. Nevertheless, Barker became convinced that Mrs Tighe had genuinely spoken of a past life.

Another case was one of several uncovered by Arnall Bloxham, of Cardiff, south Wales, an experienced hypnotherapist who was elected President of the British Society of Hypnotherapists in 1972. One of his subjects, Jane Evans, consulted him solely about a cure for rheumatism, but under hypnosis she recalled seven past lives, including one as a young Jewish mother, Rebecca, who died in a massacre of the Jews of York in 1190. She spoke of the money-lending trade practised by Jews in York and Lincoln, and of having to wear a badge to denote her religion.

At first, this detail appeared to invalidate Jane Evans's account: it was not until 1215 that Rome decreed that Jews in Christian countries should be distinguished in this way. However, Jeffrey Iverson, author of *More Lives than One* (1976), discovered that many twelfth-century Jews in England had worn the badge. Professor Barry Dobson of York University, an expert on the history of English Jews, was impressed with the tape recordings of Bloxham's sessions, stating that some of the facts given by Jane Evans and recorded on the tapes would only be known to professional historians.

There was another detail that appeared unlikely. Jane Evans described how 'Rebecca' and her children had hidden in the crypt of a church before they were discovered and killed – and, although Dobson thought he had identified the church as St Mary's in Castlegate, he said there were no churches with crypts at that time in York. And then workmen renovating St Mary's discovered… a blocked up crypt.

More recently, considerable doubt has been cast on Jane Evans's alleged recollections of past lives. In his book *Sorry You've Been Duped!* (1986), Melvin Harris dismisses them as 'clearly a fantasy… an amalgamation of at least two different stories of persecution taken from widely separated centuries'. And he quotes Professor Dobson's retraction of his earlier support for the story, which includes the opinion that the blocked-up 'crypt' is in fact a post-medieval charnel-vault.

In the same book, Harris analyses several more of Jane Evans's 'incarnations'. He discovered a number of historical novels that contained many details, both factual and fictional, appearing in her accounts. This phenomenon has been named 'cryptomnesia': the unconscious recalling of accounts that have been absorbed from reading books, seeing films or watching television. Another factor that has to be borne in mind is that the hypnotist will be (understandably) excited by the 'life' that is being revealed, and consequently his questions may unintentionally lead the subject along the lines of what he himself knows or expects to hear.

In spite of other similar setbacks, research into the possibility of reincarnation continues. Two leading workers in this field have been the American psychologists Ian Stevenson and Helen Wambach. Stevenson, Carlson Professor at the University of Virginia , a former president of the Parapsychological Association, and of the American Society for Psychical Research, documented – in *Twenty Cases Suggestive of Reincarnation* (1974) and a number of subsequent publications – examples from all over the world in which young children exhibited the ability to speak in a foreign language with which they were unfamiliar, and knew details of places they had never visited. Many had birthmarks or congenital defects that were compatible with the violent deaths they claimed to have suffered.

Helen Wambach's evidence, detailed in several books published before her death in 1983, is less persuasive. In small hypnosis workshops, her subjects were given the choice of one of ten specified periods in the past, and asked for details of their life at that time. This approach is clearly open to influence, as mentioned above, and the results she reported exhibit a vagueness and lack of specificity that cannot be substantiated by historical records.

SHAMANS

An English writer on witchcraft, Eric Maple, pointed out to the author the interesting fact that the rise of Spiritualism, the direct result of the Fox sisters' 'spirit rapping' demonstrations, occurred in 1849 – the same year as the transfer of the American Office of Indian Affairs from

*BELOW: **Shamanism was at one time widespread throughout the northern parts of Asia and America. This photograph, taken in 1910, shows an Inuit shaman in Alaska exorcising evil spirits from a sick boy.***

the Department of War to the Department of the Interior. The consequence was that the traditional ways of the native Americans began to attract more general interest, and some of the rituals of their shamans ('medicine men') – going into trance and speaking in different voices – seem to be reflected in the later practices of Spiritualist mediums.

Shamanism was at one time widespread throughout northern Asia, and its practice travelled with the first settlers across the Bering Strait into North America, encompassing the area known to zoogeographers as the Palaearctic. The shaman cured sickness, supervised sacrificial rites, and conducted the souls of the dead to the afterlife. He was able to accomplish all this by his ability to leave his body as he wished.

A Russian anthropologist recorded a detailed description from a shaman of central Siberia of the ordeals he had suffered in reaching his privileged status. He was ill with smallpox, and was so near death that he lay unconscious for three days, and was nearly buried. He saw himself descend to the underworld, after which he was transported to an island, in the middle of which stood a young birch tree reaching up to heaven. It was the tree of the Lord of the Earth, and he was given a branch to fashion himself a drum.

Mircea Eliade, who was professor of the History of Religion at the University of Chicago, has pointed out the similarity of the next stages of the shaman's progress to the symbolism used by medieval alchemists to describe their attempts to prepare the elixir of eternal life.

The shaman came to a mountain, inside which a naked man worked the bellows at a huge fire. The man caught him with a hook, and cut off his head, which was set aside so that he could observe what happened next. His

A Siberian shaman shouts and dances round his fire, beating his drum, to attain the state of ecstasy in which he was able to leave his body and visit the world of the spirits.

body was cut into pieces, and boiled in a great cauldron on the fire. When the body was reduced to a skeleton, it was forged together again on an anvil, and covered once more with flesh. The shaman recovered his senses to find himself in his tent, surrounded by his relatives, cured of his sickness, and ready to perform his function.

By putting himself into trance, the shaman was able to leave his body. He could then ascend into Heaven and make offerings to its god; he could set out to find the soul of a sick person and return it to its body; or he could conduct the soul of a dead person to its final abode. In a symbolic sense, the shaman was a man who could die, and return to life, many times.

Some Siberian peoples distinguished between 'white' and 'black' shamans. The white shaman sacrificed a horse, and, after beating his drum to reach a state of ecstasy, accompanied its soul to heaven, and there learnt if the sacrifice was acceptable, and discovered predictions of the coming weather and condition of the harvest. The black shaman descended through seven levels of the underworld, either to seek a soul and return it to a sick person, or to escort a soul to its resting place.

A report published in 1884 described a ceremony held to consign the soul of a woman who had died 40 days previously. The shaman commenced by circling his tent, beating his drum; then, entering the tent, he began to speak in a shrill falsetto voice. It was the voice of the woman, complaining that she did not know the way she was to go, and was afraid to leave her relatives. Eventually she consented to accompany the shaman, but when they reached the underworld the dead refused to accept her.

Alcohol was offered to them and, through the voice of the shaman, the dead began arguing, then singing together, and finally they accepted the woman's soul. During his return journey, alone, the shaman shouted and danced around the fire near his tent, and finally fell unconscious to the ground.

THE ASTRAL BODY

The ability to leave one's body and observe what is happening to it is not restricted to shamans. The Greek philosopher Plato (427–347 BC) believed that the soul could travel, as did many other philosophers; and, particularly during the past century, many ordinary people have reported similar incidents. These these 'out-of-body experiences' (OBEs) have become the subject of intensive study. They appear to be of two types: 'asomatic', in which the person concerned is able to view his or her environment from a different point of view, but is disembodied ('a pinpoint of

A photograph taken in 1904 shows Yebichai, a shaman in an eagle head-dress, treating a sick man who sits within a circle of feathers.

129

presence' as one put it); and 'parasomatic', in which the person appears to occupy a duplicate body.

OBEs can occur in the most banal of circumstances, as in this example of an asomatic experience:

It was summer time… and I was walking along Brentwood High Street in Essex, and there were people shopping and walking near me. As far as I can remember, I was thinking of nothing in particular when suddenly I was about 15 feet above myself, and I watched myself walking toward a cinema…I noticed the people walking round me. I suppose I walked about 30 or 40 steps, and then I was back 'inside' myself again. I felt in no way different, and just went on walking along the High Street…

A parasomatic experience can be similarly everyday:

I looked down at my second self, and found myself to be a complete replica of my material self. I touched my clothes and looked at myself, and was astounded to see that I was wearing the same black skirt, white blouse with small red spots on it, same shoes, etc… I can remember touching myself and feeling the texture of my clothing; this all felt quite solid…

One of the explanations put forward for this phenomenon is that the conscious, observing, identity is the 'astral body'. This is considered to be a third component, with the body and soul, of a sentient being. It has been described as being an exact copy of the physical body, but made of finer stuff,

THE 'ASTRAL BODY' IS CONSIDERED

TO BE A THIRD COMPONENT,

WITH THE BODY AND SOUL OF A

SENTIENT BEING…AN EXACT COPY

OF THE PHYSICAL BODY, BUT MADE

OF FINER STUFF

capable of passing through solid obstructions. A fine poetic description occurs in canto 25 of Dante's *Purgatorio*: 'Around it beams its own creative power, like to its living form in shape and size… the circumambient air adopts the shape the soul imposes on it'.

The twentieth-century French occultist Anne Osmont gave an entertaining, but dramatic, account of her first attempt at 'astral travel'. She decided to 'visit' the apartment of two friends and, after a full quarter-hour of concentration, succeeded in passing through the wall of her room. She found the couple asleep in bed, and made a mental note of what they were wearing. Thinking this was insufficient, she decided to try to leave physical evidence of her presence.

There was a gilt-decorated glass on a shelf, and she attempted to move it. She reported that it felt as heavy as a piano, but eventually it toppled from the shelf, and smashed on the floor. The couple woke with a start, and she heard the wife say, 'I bet it's that imbecile Osmont!'

When she next saw the husband, Anne Osmont told him what had happened. He confirmed the event, and said his wife was very angry, because the glass was a family heirloom. Mlle Osmont recorded that she remained physically exhausted for several days afterwards.

The American Sylvan Muldoon, author of *The Projection of the Astral Body* (1929), developed a series of exercises that enabled him to leave his physical body at will. Many other people have claimed to be able to do the same. However, most OBEs occur involuntarily, in conditions of crisis. Modern medical resuscitation techniques have made it possible to revive people who would otherwise be given up for dead, and some of the most interesting OBE reports have come from those who have been brought back from the frontiers of death.

NEAR-DEATH EXPERIENCE

In his *Republic*, Plato recounts the legend of Er the Pamphylian, who was killed in battle. His body was found some days later, and brought home for cremation, when he suddenly returned to life, and told his astonished relatives what happened after death.

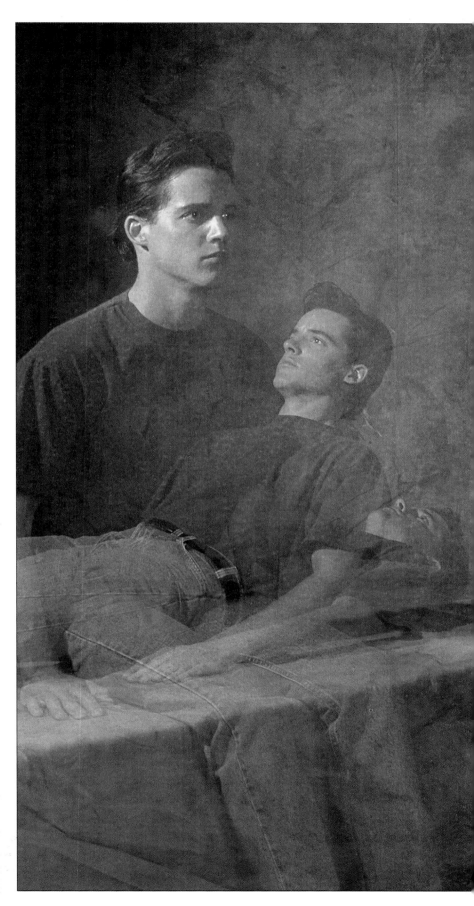

He said each soul was given the chance to choose its next incarnation – but their choice was affected by the wisdom they had acquired during life. It was an entertaining sight, 'both melancholy and ludicrous', to see how they made their decisions. Then they had to drink of the water of forgetfulness, after which they were sent back to earth like shooting stars.

Plato chose this legend as part of his argument for the separate existence of the soul, but it has echoes of the experiences of those who have been resuscitated in hospital. Literally hundreds of reports of near-death experiences (NDEs) have been published in recent years.

The striking thing, in what some of those who have been restored to life have to report, is that nearly all seem to have had a range of similar experiences. These have been classified, in order, as follows:

Calm: As soon as they realize that they are the victims of a serious accident or medical crisis, individuals experience, not panic, but peace. They may be in a speeding ambulance, or receiving urgent resuscitation in the hospital emergency room, but this only seems to increase their inner calmness.

OBE: This may be preceded by a buzzing sound, such as also been reported by those receiving general anaesthesia. Then the individual discovers, often to his or her great surprise, that they are separated from their body and floating above it. They can observe what is taking place below with cool detachment, and are often amused at the frantic activity they see – which

An artist's impression of one stage of the near-death experience: speeding down a black tunnel towards a brilliant light.

they subsequently can describe. Frequently they find they can move about the room and listen to whispered conversations – and emergency medical staff are, apparently, able to confirm later that these conversations took place.

The Black Tunnel: People next discover that they are speeding down a long dark tunnel toward a brilliant light. This is a far from daunting experience, and some people find it ecstatically exciting.

The Being of Light: As they emerge from the tunnel into the brilliance, the dying persons are greeted by a Being – frequently of no specific individuality, although some people have identified Christ or the Virgin Mary, and who is said to 'radiate love and compassion', and who undertakes to be their guide.

The Garden: The Being leads them into a beautiful garden, with running brooks and brightly coloured flowers, all bathed in brilliant sunlight. They are sometimes accompanied by mysterious music, which those of a literary turn of mind have described as 'the music of the spheres'. There have also been reports of a 'city of light', built of glass or crystal and suffused with a golden glow.

The Life Review: The individual is shown a 'replay' of his or her whole life, and realizes the opportunities that have been missed in the spiritual betterment of the self, and of other people. This is reminiscent of the experience of those rescued from drowning, who have often reported seeing 'their whole lives passing before them in a second'.

The Vision of Knowledge: The dying person is offered a brief glimpse of 'another realm of reality, in which all knowledge seems to co-exist beyond time and space'.

Meeting Others: Relatives and friends who have died are encountered, among them some whom the individual did not know were dead – although this is often found, later, to be true. They may say that it is not yet time for the individual to remain with them, and occasionally people will be told that they must return, because they have left a task undone, or someone who must be looked after.

The Return: After what has been experienced, the news that the individual must return

usually provokes intense disappointment; he or she may beg to be allowed to stay, but the Being insists that this is not possible. Soon after, the person is pronounced alive, and in due course regains consciousness.

One case that has provoked particular interest is that of Durdana Khan, a two-year-old child in Pakistan in 1968. She contracted a severe virus infection, and passed into coma. Her father, an army doctor, tried to revive her, but could discover no signs of life. For 15 minutes he battled, all the time saying under his breath, 'Come back, my child, come back!' At last, Durdana recovered consciousness.

Shortly after, her mother asked her, 'Where have you been when you went away from

Those who emerge from the black tunnel are greeted by a radiant Being of Light. J.M.W. Turner's Angel Standing in the Sun.

133

Mummy?' 'To the stars' said the little girl. She described entering a beautiful garden, meeting her maternal grandmother and other relations, and talking to God. God told her that her father was calling her, and that she must go back. Later, it is said, she saw photographs of dead relatives for the first time, and identified them.

Some ten years later, after the Khans had moved to London, Durdana appeared on television to recount her experiences, and show pictures of the garden she had subsequently painted from memory. One viewer, an old lady, was astounded to recognize it, and a meeting with Durdana was arranged. The lady had 'died' briefly while in a Nazi concentration camp, and she not only agreed with Durdana on the details, but was able to tell her 'what is was like round the next corner'.

Not all near-death experiences are pleasant, however. One 23-year-old girl who had taken an overdose of sleeping pills described what she felt and saw as she was being rushed, unconscious, to hospital in an ambulance:

I felt hotter and hotter and there was a sort of gritty feeling behind my eyelids…It seemed to me that I opened my eyes and saw I was in a huge glowing cavern deep under the earth… the ground was like coal. I could only shuffle about…somewhere there was a huge booming sound like machinery, and for some reason it filled me with the worst dread I have ever experienced. Then through some pillars of coal I could just make out a tall figure of infinite kindness…he looked over at me, smiled, and went away…I started screaming and sobbing for him to come and take me with him…it was the worst feeling of all, utter desolation…then suddenly I gave a huge jump and realized I was having my face slapped. I was back, alive, and I sobbed with joy.

> ONE THOUGHT, IN PARTICULAR, MIGHT OCCUR TO THE READER OF THESE ACCOUNTS: THE EXPERIENCES SEEM TO BE VERY MUCH WHAT THE INDIVIDUAL MIGHT EXPECT TO OCCUR AFTER THE MOMENT OF DEATH

One thought, in particular, may occur to the reader of these accounts: the experiences seem to be very much what the individual might expect to occur after the moment of death. It is certainly true that those who 'return' speak of having undergone a spiritual enlightenment, and frequently make radical changes to their way of life – but this, in view of the traumatic nature of their experience, is hardly surprising.

Many of those who have collected accounts of NDEs cite them as firm evidence of a specific life after death. But there is a major obstacle

This drawing by William Blake (1757–1827) of The Death of the Good Old Man reflects the concept of the soul being borne away by angelic spirits, but it also captures some of the feelings and emotions that patients report during the near-death experience.

to this contention: none of these witnesses – in terms of the definition made in Chapter 1 – has actually died. They have been very near death, and they have had experiences, or 'visions', that are dramatic, and probably reflect what they have been told the afterlife is like, but not one of them has suffered the ultimate cessation of the vital functions.

There is no question that NDEs are 'real', in the sense that they are genuine mental experiences, and medical experts have made a number of efforts to explain them. In most cases, these are attempts, without physiological justification, to explain away the phenomenon.

THERE IS NO QUESTION THAT NDEs ARE 'REAL', IN THE SENSE THAT THEY ARE GENUINE MENTAL EXPERIENCES, AND MEDICAL EXPERTS HAVE MADE A NUMBER OF EFFORTS TO EXPLAIN THEM

Dr Melvin Morse, a paediatrician of Seattle – whose book, *Closer to the Light* (1990), was a study of NDEs in young children – has, however, put forward a plausible theory. In *Is There Life After Death?* (1995), Professor Robert Kastenbaum, an American clinical psychologist, summarises Dr Morse's propositions:

1: Previous investigations have shown that electrical stimulation of the temporal lobe of the brain can produce spontaneous recall, the sound of music, visions associated with religious belief, OBEs and other 'hallucinations'.

2: There is a direct link between the temporal lobe and the mid-brain, particularly the hippocampus. Structures in the mid-brain are known to be essential in the processing of information, and the evocation of memories and dreams. This is the part of the brain, as Morse puts it, 'most associated with a sense of consciousness, or soul'.

3: When an individual is under psychological stress – or under the influence of psychoactive drugs – neurochemical changes occur in the mid-brain. This results in a change in the level of the chemical serotonin, which is believed to influence mood. Drugs such as LSD, for instance, alter serotonin levels and induce hallucinations.

4: Emotionally stressful situations – such as close brushes with death – and the resultant release of serotonin, affect a specific set of neurons in the temporal lobe, and the subsequent relaxation of control produces OBEs and hallucinations. The potential for NDEs, and other altered states of consciousness, therefore always exists within the brain.

Dr Morse went on to consider the often discussed distinction between the left and right temporal lobes of the brain. Normally, the left temporal lobe seems to be the part of the brain concerned with 'everyday' activities. Morse wrote:

When we reveal the right temporal lobe as the place in the brain where the NDE occurs, we are talking about the spot where the mind, body and spirit interact. We are talking about the area that houses the very spark of life itself.

CHEATING DEATH

And, finally, what of those who have hoped to escape the clutches of death? From time immemorial, as an explanation of the immortality of the gods, myths have told of a secret potion or powder – an 'elixir' – that would confer everlasting life, or even eternal youth.

The Arabic legend of al-Khidr ('the green') can be traced back to Babylonian myth. It tells how al-Khidr set out on a quest to find the ultimate secrets of life, and came to a rock that shone with a blinding white light, 'A voice from heaven called to him, "Proceed onwards and drink, for verily it is the fount of life. Be made clean and pure, and then you will live until the day of the Last Trump, when all in heaven and earth will die, and you taste of final death." So he advanced until he reached the summit of the rock, and found a spring wherein descended heavenly water. He drank of it, and was made pure and clean.'

The fact that gold, alone among the metals known until the nineteenth century, was indestructible and remained shiny in all conditions, led many people to the belief that it was somehow connected with eternal life. The continuing quest of the medieval alchemists for the Philosopher's Stone had two ends: not only would it transmute baser metals into gold, but it would also confer immortality on its possessor. Popular legends credited at least two alchemists, Nicolas Flamel (1330–1418) and the Count St Germain (*c.* 1700–80), with having achieved this doubtfully happy condition.

It is a development in twentieth-century science that has seemed to offer some people the possibility of cheating death. If human sperm and ova, and tissue samples, can be preserved apparently indefinitely by deep-freezing, they argue, is it not possible that the entire body could be preserved in the same way? Maybe,

The incorruptibility of gold gave it a magical appeal to many early peoples. Here the features of a dead person are preserved for eternity in a Syrian funerary mask from the first century AD.

some time in the future, medical science will have advanced so far that ways will be found of restoring the frozen body to life?

Cryonics – the freezing and storing of the dead – is an expensive business, because it requires that the deceased must leave sufficient funds in his or her will to ensure maintenance of the body for an indefinite time. Nevertheless, more than 1,000 people subscribe to various cryonics societies in the United States. In 1993, the cost of full-body preservation was $120,000. Preservation of the head alone cost a mere $50,000 – but this necessitates belief in the possibility that future scientists will find some way of producing a new body, possibly by cloning.

As soon as death occurs, resuscitation is applied

until the body can be connected to a heart-lung machine, which also rapidly cools the blood by some 20°C (68°F). Injections of blood-thinners and other chemicals are made, and the body then spends two days in a bath of silicone oil as it is cooled to -90°C (-130°F). It is then wrapped in two padded bags, placed in an aluminium container, and lowered into a bath of liquid nitrogen, which reduces the temperature to -220°C (-364°F). Then it must be maintained at this temperature, for as long as is necessary!

The first person to undergo cryonic preservation was Dr James H. Bedford, a 73-year-old California professor of psychology, in 1967. Although Walt Disney, who died in 1966, was rumoured to have had his body preserved in the

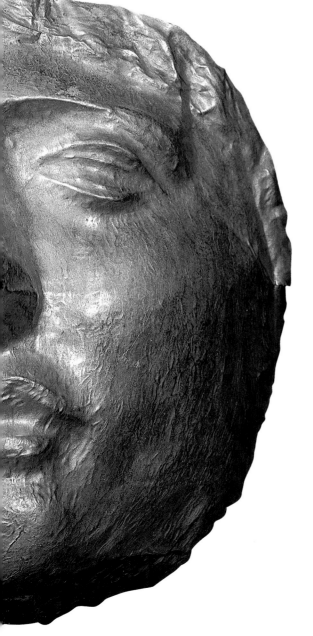

same way. But, as presenter Greg Palmer commented in the American television feature *Death: the Trip of a Lifetime*: 'Walt was obviously a big resurrection fan, but he was far too romantic for the freezer. I suspect he's really in a glass coffin hidden in a cavern beneath Space Mountain. And there he waits, not for science, but a kiss.' In fact, Disney was cremated, and his ashes deposited at Forest Lawn in Glendale (see page 88).

Critics of cryonics point out that no major human organ has ever been preserved by freezing at such low temperatures: the tissues are split open by ice crystals. And, as Greg Palmer, who visited the Alcor Life Extension Foundation in the course of preparing his television programme, reported, 'Nobody I talked to… claims anything other than a slim chance for success, no matter how much you pay or pay. What they do emphasise is that a slim chance is better than no chance.'

But for most of us, without the necessary funds, there is no chance. Whether there is life after death remains a mystery until we, perhaps, experience it. The English poet and playwright John Gay (1685–1732) shall have the last word, in the epitaph he wrote for himself:

Life is a jest; and all things show it.
I thought so once; but now I know it.

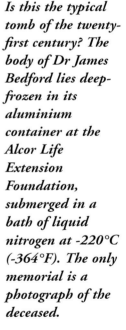

Is this the typical tomb of the twenty-first century? The body of Dr James Bedford lies deep-frozen in its aluminium container at the Alcor Life Extension Foundation, submerged in a bath of liquid nitrogen at -220°C (-364°F). The only memorial is a photograph of the deceased.

137

CHAPTER 8

THE
UNQUIET DEAD

'Is there a life before death?' a nightclub comic once asked. His question was meant to be ironic, but there does, in fact, appear to a strangely undefined zone between what we know as life, and what has been identified in the previous chapters as death.

The British Society for Psychical Research (SPR) was founded in London in 1882, its aims being defined as 'to examine without prejudice or prepossession and in a scientific manner those faculties of man, real or supposed, which appear to be inexplicable on any generally recognised hypothesis'. This could well be considered a catch-all definition, but the SPR's founders knew what they were after: investigation of all the phenomena associated with Spiritualism (see page 118) as well as such related subjects as telepathy and clairvoyance, altered states of consciousness, and – the subject of their first significant enquiry – phantasms of the living.

Among the founding and early members of the SPR were a number of distinguished academics including: Henry Sidgwick (1838–1900), Professor of Moral Philosophy at Cambridge, the society's first president; his wife Eleanor (1845–1936), Principal of Newnham College, Cambridge; Sir William Barrett (1844–1925), Professor of Physics at University College, Dublin; Sir Oliver Lodge (1831–1940), Professor of Physics at Liverpool University; Lord Rayleigh (1842–1919), head of the Cavendish Laboratory in Cambridge; J.J. Thomson (1856–1940), who succeeded Lord Rayleigh at the Cavendish; and Sir William Crookes FRS (1832–1919) – a formidable gathering of intellects.

In 1886 three active members of the SPR, Edmund Gurney, Frederic Myers and Frank Podmore, produced the Society's first major publication, the massive two-volume *Phantasms of the Living*. Much of the evidence cited in this work was about telepathy between living persons, but it included 13 first-hand and well-attested cases of what came to be called 'crisis apparitions'. This was defined as a

FACING PAGE: The idea of the 'undead' has proved a fertile source for film-makers. F. W. Murnau's **Nosferatu** *(1921) featured Max Schreck as Count Orlok, and was the first in a long line of vampire films.*

LEFT: The distinguished physicist Sir Oliver Lodge and his wife. Lodge was a founder member of the SPR, and became a convinced Spiritualist after he was sure that he had established communication with his dead son Raymond, killed in World War 1.

hallucination of someone who, it would later transpire, had died no more than twelve hours before or after.

Struck by these accounts, the SPR later carried out a more extensive survey, supervised by Sidgwick himself, who published *A Report on the Census of Hallucinations* in the Society's *Journal* in 1894. This census was based on some 17,000 questionnaires that had been completed in the course of the enquiry, in which 300 people reported experiencing visual hallucinations of a person known to them; and, of these, 80 coincided, within 12 hours, with that person's death.

This was the first serious investigation of a phenomenon – and one that must be distinguished from traditional sightings of ghosts – that had been occasionally reported for centuries. One of the more detailed early accounts was by Daniel Defoe (1660–1731), who published it in 1706. He explained, 'This thing has very much affected me, and I am well satisfied as I am of the best grounded Matter of Fact. And why should we dispute Matter of Fact, because we cannot solve things, of which we have no certain or demonstrative Notions, seems strange to me… '

The story concerned a Mrs Bargrave, living in Canterbury, Kent, She had previously lived in Dover, some 15 miles (24 kilometres) away, where she was close friends with a Mrs Veal who still lived there. On the morning of 8 September 1705, as the clock struck noon, Mrs Veal, wearing riding clothes, appeared at Mrs Bargrave's door. They were about to kiss, when 'Mrs Veal drew her hand across her own Eyes, and said, I am not very well, and so waved it.'

The two ladies talked for some time, and Mrs Veal reminded Mrs Bargrave of the books they used to read together, particularly Drelincourt's *Book of Death* which, she said, had given her great comfort. 'Then she said, she would not take her Leave of her, and walk'd from Mrs Bargrave in her view, till a turning interrupted the sight of her… '

Defoe reported that Mrs Veal had died, 'of her Fits', at noon on 7 September – exactly 24 hours before she appeared at Mrs Bargrave's door.

One of the cases reported to the SPR in their census had occurred some 30 years previously. The writer. G.F. Russell, was a youth of 19 in 1855, at a time his elder brother Oliver was serving in the Crimean War as a lieutenant with the 7th Royal Fusiliers. Oliver's latest letter had said that he was not well, and in low spirits; his brother wrote back to say that, if anything happened to him, he should try to appear in their room, 'where we had often as boys sat together and indulged in a surreptitious pipe and chat.'

On the night of 8/9 September, Russell reported:

Ghosts, too, have provided film-makers with a fund of inspiration. In this 1938 film of Dickens's **A Christmas Carol,** *Reginald Owen, as Scrooge, speaks with the ghost of his erstwhile business partner Marley, played by Leo G. Carroll.*

I awoke suddenly and saw, facing the window of my room, by my bedside, surrounded by a light sort of phosphorescent mist as it were, my brother kneeling... I had not been thinking or dreaming of him, and indeed had forgotten all about what I had written to him. I decided it must be fancy... but on looking up there he was again... The apparition turned his head slowly and again looked anxiously and lovingly at me, and I saw then for the first time a wound in the right temple with a red stream from it...

Russell later learnt that Oliver had been given his letter as he was about to receive the sacrament from a chaplain, before going forward in the storming of the defences of Sevastopol. The chaplain confirmed that he had opened and read the letter. Oliver had just led his men inside the walls of the citadel when a bullet hit him in the right temple. He fell against a pile of other dead men, 'where he was found 36 hours afterward. His death took place, or rather he fell, though he may not have died immediately, on 8 September 1855.'

There were numerous reports of such crisis apparitions in the years following the SPR's census, and similar censuses were produced by associated societies in France, Germany and the United States. The characteristics the apparitions all shared were that they occurred only close to the time of death, and that each death was sudden and sometimes violent – a crisis.

Many theories have been advanced to explain the phenomena. It is perhaps unfortunate that the SPR should have described them as 'hallucinations', in view of the general use of this word to mean false ideas and images that spring solely from a disordered mind. This, no doubt, was due to caution on the part of the scientific members of the Society in making their findings public. One of the explanations put forward was that the apparitions were 'astral bodies' (see page 129); another, that they were

genuine spirits of the dead. However, they generally appeared to only one person, a family member or close friend, and, most importantly, within some twelve hours either side of the moment of death.

This suggests that the apparitions were the result of some kind of telepathic communication between the dying person and the recipient – and the delay that often occurs after demise lends colour to the belief that the personality survives intact, and strongly active, even after death.

Most crisis apparitions are silent, but there are cases (as in that of Mrs Bargrave and Mrs Veal) in which a conversation takes place. In his book *Apparitions* (1943), G.N.M. Tyrell, an SPR member, proposed that the physical appearance of the apparition, and any exchange of words, was a projection from the mind of the percipient, based on the telepathic information received. The case of David M'Connel supports this theory.

Lieutenant M'Connel was an RAF officer, who had previously flown for the Royal Navy Air Service. Shortly before 3.30 on the

THE CHARACTERISTICS THAT ALL CRISIS APPARITIONS SHARE IS THAT THEY OCCUR ONLY CLOSE TO THE TIME OF DEATH AND THAT EACH DEATH IS SUDDEN

A considerable number of cases of crisis apparitions have occurred in wartime, when the emotions of the dying person are particularly highly charged.

afternoon of 7 December 1918, he crashed his plane in thick fog some 50 miles (80 kilometres) from his station at Scampton in Lincolnshire, and was killed. At that time, Lieutenant J.J. Larkin was sitting in his room at Scampton:

I heard someone walking up the passage; the door opened with the usual noise and clatter that David always made; I heard his 'Hello, boy!' and I turned half round in my chair and saw him standing in the doorway, half in and half out of the room…

He was dressed in his full flying clothes, but wearing his naval cap, there being nothing unusual in his appearance… In reply to his 'Hello, boy!' I remarked, 'Hello, back already?' He replied: 'Yes, got there all right, had a good trip'. I was looking at him the whole time he was speaking. He said, 'Well, cheerio!', closed the door noisily, and went out.

Lieutenant Garner-Smith confirmed that Larkin told him, shortly before 3.45, that M'Connel had returned, and they did not learn of his death until that evening. M'Connel found

his flying helmet uncomfortable, and always carried his naval cap with him, to change into as soon as he landed – but he was wearing his flying helmet when he died. Larkin, while confident that he had seen the apparition, presumably imagined what he would have expected in normal circumstances – M'Connel wearing his cap, and announcing that he had had 'a good trip'.

The three cases cited have all been of apparitions that made their appearance at the moment of death, or shortly after. Examples of prior apparitions are rarer, but one account is particularly dramatic.

Squadron-Leader (later Wing-Commander) George Potter was serving in Egypt with an RAF bomber group occupied with torpedo and mine-laying operations in the eastern Mediterranean during World War II. 'Too many times I had known beyond doubt that a man would die soon and, hunch or not, my predictions as to "who" and "when" were always uncannily accurate.'

One night, Potter was drinking in the mess with Flying Officer Reg Lamb, close to the Wing-Commander of one of the squadrons:

Tony O'Rahilly was sent to photograph a fire at Wem Town Hall in Shropshire in 1995. One picture appeared to reveal the figure of a girl to the right of the stairs. It has been suggested that there could be a connection with a conflagration at Wem in 1677, when a young girl set fire to a thatched roof with a candle.

There was a burst of laughter from the group on my left, and I glanced toward them. Then I saw it. I saw the head and shoulders of the Wing-Commander moving ever so slowly in a bottomless depth of blue-blackness. His lips were drawn back from this teeth in a dreadful grin; he had eye sockets but no eyes; the flesh of his face was dully blotched in greenish, purplish shadows, with shreds peeling off near his left ear.

Lamb told Potter that he had gone deathly white, and 'looked as if he'd seen a ghost'. Some hours later, the squadron flew off to mine the shipping approaches to Benghazi, and in the evening Potter was told that the Wing-Commander's plane had been shot down – but that he and his crew had been seen getting into their dinghies: 'I felt an enormous sense of relief… but my elation was short-lived. They searched, but no one ever saw [them] again. The blue-black nothingness was the Mediterranean at night; and he was floating somewhere in it, with just his head and shoulders held up by his Mae West.'

GHOSTS

There is credible evidence – and, indeed, a plausible explanation – for the appearance of crisis apparitions. When it comes to ghosts, however, the evidence is frequently more tenuous, and the explanations harder to justify. For one thing, even the word 'ghost' can have different meanings for different people. When, a half-century ago, Professor H.H. Price of Oxford University was asked 'Do you believe in ghosts?', he could only reply that the question could not be answered until the term was defined. In other words, as one of Price's contemporaries, Professor C.E.M. Joad, might famously have remarked: 'It all depends upon what you mean by ghost'.

Nevertheless, in popular use, the characteristics of a ghost are generally agreed. It is (supposedly) the surviving presence of a being, who may be recently dead, or long gone. It may make its presence felt by an unnatural lowering of temperature, the sound of a wind or

the fluttering of birds' wings, strange smells or sounds, the movement of objects – even, in the most dramatic cases, appearing as a shadow, a misty wraith, or an apparently solid body.

Ancient peoples firmly believed that many spirits remained close to their place of death or burial, and more primitive cultures still do so (see page 98). In *Phaedo* Plato wrote:

You know the stories about souls that… roam about tombs and burial grounds in the neighbourhood of which, as they say, ghostly phantoms of souls have actually been seen; just the sort of apparitions that souls like that might produce, souls that are not pure when they are released, but still keep some of that visible substance, which explains why they can be seen… It is clearly not the souls of the good but those of the wicked that are compelled to wander about such places, as the penalty for a bad way of life in the past.

This view of ghosts – as those who are denied their final rest in death because they have not expunged the consequences of their actions in life – brings them closer to crisis apparitions, but there is still a significant difference. The appearance of ghosts, whether visibly or otherwise, can occur long after the death of the persons concerned, and they can, it seems, be experienced by numbers of people who have no connection or acquaintance with their history.

In Hong Kong, a man makes offerings of food and incense during the Yue Lang ('hungry ghosts') festival, when the spirits of those who have died by violence or neglect have to be fed and provided for to prevent their revengeful return.

Raynham Hall in Norfolk is reputedly haunted by the ghost of the 'Brown Lady'. In 1936, two photographers from **Country Life** *reported that they had seen her on the staircase, and produced this photograph in confirmation.*

One evening some six weeks after moving in, Rosina saw the figure of a tall lady, in a dress of soft black wool, who stood at the head of the stairs and then descended them. The figure's face was hidden by a handkerchief held in her right hand: 'The whole impression was that of a lady in widow's weeds. There was no cap on the head but a general effect of blackness suggests a bonnet, with a long veil or hood.'

Over the next two years, Rosina saw the figure some half-dozen times, but told no one else, except a friend to whom she wrote occasional letters. During the summer of 1882 her elder married sister saw it once; in autumn 1883 the cook and a housemaid saw it together; and in December 1883 Rosina's six-year-old brother and a friend saw the figure through a window, and 'ran in to see who it could be that was crying so bitterly'.

After the first sighting, Rosina would follow the figure downstairs, where it would stand for some time at a window, before going along a passage to the garden door and disappearing. She tried speaking to it, even attempted to touch or seize it, but it always eluded her. The only sounds she heard were footsteps, 'very light, you can hardly hear it, except on the linoleum, and then only like a person walking softly with thin boots on'. During May and June 1884 she tried fastening thin threads across the stairs, and twice saw the figure pass right through them.

In July and August 1884 the appearances became more frequent, and the footsteps were heard by Rosina's three younger sisters, and also by the cook, who then reported that she had twice seen 'a lady in a widow's dress, with her face hidden in a handkerchief in her right hand'. And on 6 August, a neighbour sent to enquire after a woman he had seen crying in the garden.

Four days later, Rosina and a younger sister saw the figure together, for more than ten minutes, and shortly after both her elder sister, another younger sister and a parlour maid reported it. During this time, the footsteps were often heard at night, by the family, servants and visitors; 'in all, about twenty people, many of them not having previously heard of the apparition or sounds'.

All the same, there appears to be a certain similarity with crisis apparitions, in that this history frequently involves a highly emotional event, such as great sorrow, the omission of a proper burial or death by violence.

One such case reported to the SPR was notable for the number of people who saw the ghost, and the frequency with which it was seen. In April 1882, the Despard family moved into a substantial house on Pittville Circus Road, Cheltenham, in England. Their second-eldest daughter was 19-year-old Rosina, a calmly objective, scientifically minded young woman who subsequently trained as a doctor, and wrote a detailed account of her experiences.

After consulting Frederic Myers of the SPR, Rosina kept a camera ready, but on the few occasions when she was able to use it the lighting was insufficient for the photographic plates then available to work. Gradually, the appearances of the figure decreased in number, and it was not seen again after 1889. Rosina wrote, 'Up to about 1886 it was so solid and lifelike that it was often mistaken for a real person... At all times it intercepted the light... The upper part of the figure always left a more distinct impression than the lower, but this may partly be due to the fact that one naturally looks at people's faces before their feet.'

The Despard family made enquiries about previous occupiers of the house. From 1860 until 1876, they discovered, the occupant had been a Mr Swinhoe, and Rosina concluded that the ghost was that of his second wife, Imogen, who died two years after her husband, and was buried in a cemetery about a quarter of a mile away from the house.

With such an explanation, one may wonder why the appearances ceased after seven years. There is evidence to suggest that it is the intensity of the emotion that determines the survival of a ghostly presence. Longleat, the Wiltshire seat of the Marquess of Bath, has long been said to be haunted by a ghost with a grim history – the 'Green Lady'. A figure in an agony of grief, she stalks a gallery high in the house, and some of those who have seen her – as well as some of those who have only felt her presence in the gallery – have experienced such pain and terror that they have been unable to remain in the building.

The ghost is said to be that of Lady Louisa Carteret, daughter of the Earl of Granville and wife of the second Viscount Weymouth. Lord Weymouth (like many of his successors) is said to have been of an uncertain temper; the marriage was not a happy one, and Lady Louisa took a lover.

According to the family legend, Lord Weymouth returned one day to Longleat without warning, and surprised his wife and her lover together. Swords were drawn, and the two men fought together the length of the gallery, with only the terrified Lady Louisa as witness, until at last Lord Weymouth thrust his rival through. Quickly and in secret, he dragged the body down to the cellars, and buried it there.

After this, the guilty Lord Weymouth abandoned Longleat, leaving the estate to decay into an overgrown wilderness. Whether he left the distraught Lady Louisa to live in near-isolation there is unsure; she died in 1736, and he not until 1751. It was shortly after his death that the ghost was first reported, when his son (later the first Marquess) returned to restore the dilapidated property.

There is no documentary evidence to support this story – but, early in the twentieth century, a grisly discovery was made at Longleat. While a central heating system was being installed by a team of workmen, some flagstones in the cellar had to be raised to facilitate the laying of some pipes. Under them lay the bones of a young man, dressed in jackboots and clothes of the early eighteenth century. If there truly is a ghost, and it is that of Lady Louisa, then her lasting presence may be attributed to the intense terror and guilt she felt – and that her vengeful husband would have caused her to continue to feel – until her early death.

A photograph taken by moonlight, on Mount Royd Estate, Bradford, in 1997. What appear to be two ghostly heads can been seen floating at the centre of the picture.

It is difficult to advance a scientific explanation for phenomena of this kind. The experience of those who report seeing, hearing or feeling the presence of something supernatural is, after all, purely subjective. Occasionally, photographs of what are claimed to be ghostly appearances have been put forward. However, in nearly every case these 'appearances' were not seen at the time, but only discovered by accident when the film was developed. 'Ghost hunters' claim to have recorded sudden and inexplicable changes of temperature, or strange sounds, but these are only marginally persuasive.

There is no physical effect, currently known, that could account for the appearance of ghosts. Some people, by an analogy with tape recording, have suggested that the personality of the dead person, and the events that he or she experienced, is somehow 'impressed' on the surroundings, and can be heard or seen by people particularly 'in tune'.

Another theory is that there is some kind of 'field of force', hitherto undetected by scientific investigation, in which intense emotion creates a turbulence – a vortex – that can persist for some time. The intensity of the emotion would determine the strength of the vortex, and therefore how long a period would pass before it faded away. If transmission in this field of force could also account for telepathy, the theory would successfully bring together this phenomena with those of crisis apparitions and ghosts.

RIGHT: *The belief that ghosts exist can be found in all corners of the world. In Benin, ghosts are known as* egunguns, *and it is said that they revisit Earth at certain times of the year and take possession of living people. Here a Benin magician, possessed by the spirit of an* egungun, *dances wildly within a circle of villagers.*

VOICES FROM THE DEAD

Claims have been made in recent years for a discovery that, if genuine, could be taken as giving some support to the theory advanced above. The possibility that radio might be used to communicate with the dead was first put forward by Thomas Edison in 1920, in an interview he gave to *Scientific American* magazine. He said that he intended to build equipment that would be 'as valuable to the psychic researcher as the microscope is to the scientist'. But little more was heard of it before his death in 1931.

It was nearly thirty years later, in 1959, that a Russian-born artist and film-producer, named Friedrich Jürgenson, took his tape recorder into the remote Swedish countryside to record birdsong. When he played back the tape, he found he could also hear faint voices, speaking in Swedish and Norwegian. At first he thought that he had recorded a stray radio broadcast, but he subsequently identified the voices as those of dead relatives and friends.

Jürgenson carried out experiments over the next few years, and published the results in *Voices from the Universe* (1964). It attracted the attention of the German parapsychologist Hans Bender, and also that of Dr Konstantin Raudive, former professor of psychology at Uppsala University. Both men carried out independent controlled experiments, and became convinced that factory-clean tapes, run through a tape recorder in a silent environment, could record human voices speaking intelligible words. Raudive and Jürgenson worked together on the project until 1969, when they quarrelled.

Raudive continued the work, and made more than 100,000 recordings. He claimed to recognize many of the voices, and said that some

THE GERMAN PARAPSYCHOLOGIST HANS BENDER AND DR KONSTANTIN RAUDIVE BOTH BECAME CONVINCED THAT FACTORY-CLEAN TAPES, RUN THROUGH A TAPE RECORDER IN A SILENT ENVIRONMENT, COULD RECORD HUMAN VOICES SPEAKING INTELLIGIBLE WORDS

– including Adolf Hitler, Carl Jung and Goethe – identified themselves. He published a book in 1968, which included a small disc containing samples of the voices he had recorded.

The book was brought to the attention of a British publisher, who brought out an English-language edition, entitled *Breakthrough*, in 1971. Before the new edition was published, he set up a series of sophisticated experiments. To avoid the suggestion that the voices came from everyday radio broadcasts, some of the recordings were made inside a 'Faraday cage', which would screen out all radio frequencies, and the tests were supervised by a team of electronics experts and recording engineers.

It was reported that over 200 voices were heard on the tapes, some so clear that they were intelligible to everybody who heard them. The publisher's chairman was confident that he had identified the voice of an old friend, the pianist Artur Schnabel, and on one tape Dr Raudive himself was addressed by his childhood nickname.

Raudive kept up his experiments until his death in September 1974. Ten days later, Hans Bender was present at a conference on the paranormal in Germany. A tape-recorder was set up, in the hope that Raudive would provide confirmation of his existence in the afterlife. Some of those present claimed that they heard his voice, but little that was intelligible.

Various theories have been advanced to account for these 'Raudive voices'. One of the more attractive is that they are somehow recorded on the tape by some kind of involuntary psychokinesis on the part of the experimenter, who is receiving the information by telepathy. This would account for the voices speaking only in languages with which the experimenter is familiar.

POLTERGEISTS

One type of 'ghostly' activity that does not seem to be associated with the manifestation of a particular dead person, or centred upon a specific site, is what is generally known as a 'poltergeist'. The word was originally used in German folklore, being compounded from *polter*, meaning a noisy racket, and *geist* – which, although probably the origin of the word 'ghost', meant in this context elf or goblin.

The term was adopted during the nineteenth century, by SPR investigators and the Italian criminologist Cesare Lombroso, to describe a wide range of apparently supernatural events – the moving of domestic articles, flinging of stones and other objects (some of them from an unknown source), apparent 'teleportation' of articles into closed rooms, and the production of all kinds of noises, such as rapping, banging or scratching, or even the sound of human whistling, singing or talking.

Accounts of poltergeist activity have been recorded for many centuries. In 1135, for example, Provost Nicholas of Le Mans, France, was awakened by 'uproar and fearful noises, as if a spirit had thrown enormous stones against the walls, with a force that shook the roof, walls and ceilings'. Other strange events followed – plates were moved from one place to another; a candle burst into flame 'though very far from the fire'; and when meals were placed on the table, bran, ashes or soot were scattered over them, so that they could not be eaten. Provost Nicholas's wife, who had spun some thread to weave, found it 'twisted and ravelled in such a way, that all who saw it could not sufficiently admire the manner in which it was done'.

Convinced the household was being attacked by an evil spirit, Nicholas sent for priests, who sprinkled holy water about the place. But the next night a voice was heard, 'as it were the voice of a young girl, who, with sighs that seemed drawn from the bottom of her heart, said in a lamentable voice that her name was Garnier; and addressing herself to Provost Nicholas, said:

Alas! whence do I come? from what distant country, through how many storms, dangers, through snow, cold, fire and bad weather, have I arrived at this place! I have not received power to harm any one – but prepare yourselves with the sign of the cross against a band of evil spirits, who are here only to do you harm; have a mass of the Holy Ghost said for me, and a mass for the defunct; and you, my dear sister-in-law, give some clothes to the poor for me.

This account comes from Augustine Calmet's book, *Le Monde Fantôme*, and was written some six centuries after the occurrence, so the details are suspect. Although the poltergeist activity is typical of many more recent events, there are no other cases in which such a long, clearly intelligible speech was made. It seems most likely that some woman in the room – possibly Nicholas's wife Amica – went into trance, somehow communicating with a dead person, and this is an edited version of what she said.

> THE WORD 'POLTERGEIST' IS USED TO DESCRIBE A WIDE RANGE OF APPARENTLY SUPERNATURAL EVENTS – THE MOVING OF DOMESTIC ARTICLES, FLINGING OF STONES AND OTHER OBJECTS... AND THE PRODUCTION OF ALL KINDS OF NOISES

FACING PAGE: The local priest stands amazed in this somewhat imaginative illustration of poltergeist activity in Cideville, France, in 1851.

BELOW: The distinguished Italian criminologist Cesare Lombroso (1836–1909) was one of the first to employ the term 'poltergeist'. He investigated a number of cases, including the ability of the medium Eusapia Palladino to move objects, apparently without touching them.

RIGHT: Englishman, Harry Price, the self-styled 'ghost hunter', was the most prominent investigator of psychical phenomena during the middle years of the twentieth century. Here he draws chalk rings round the bases of objects to determine whether they move during his investigation of a 'haunted' house.

BELOW: Two of the children involved in the Enfield case – obviously unharmed and enjoying the publicity – lie on the bedroom floor, allegedly tumbled out of bed by the poltergeist.

In all other respects, these and similar phenomena have been repeated hundreds of times in succeeding centuries. But, in most cases, there is a common factor that may well invalidate any suggestion that the events have a connection with life after death – or, indeed, with any supernatural agency. Quite early in the twentieth century, investigators remarked that poltergeist activity seemed to be connected with the presence in the household of a pubescent girl who had recently begun to menstruate. Occasionally, it was a male youth of a similar age.

This is a time when many adolescents begin to lose the innate confidence of younger children, and start to question their identity. They may try to re-establish their sense of self by acts of aggression, or other ways of drawing attention to themselves. In a number of recent cases, investigators have incontestably show that 'poltergeist' events have been the result of unconscious, or deliberate, fraud on the part of young teenagers.

Parents and friends are, of course, unwilling to believe that these youngsters are the agents of seemingly inexplicable happenings. In a 1998 case in France, for example, parapsychologists from the University of Toulouse were called in to examine a 'spirit' that answered questions by rapping 'yes' or 'no' on the house wall. All too soon, they discovered that the rappings only

occurred when the 11-year-old son of the family was sitting on a sofa that touched the wall. He quickly confessed.

Nevertheless, it is often difficult to convince inexperienced witnesses that there is a simple explanation for what they have observed. For instance, in the case of the 'Enfield poltergeist' in north London in 1977, a passing tradesman testified that he had seen, through an upstairs window, the young daughter of the household (who had just begun to menstruate) 'floating horizontally across the room'. But a surreptitious video recording made at the time showed her 'bouncing up and down on the bed, making little flapping movements with both hands'.

Seemingly unexplained events such as this will inevitably cause acute distress to the family concerned, and to their neighbours. Unable to detect the cause, they will frequently attribute them to the influence of an 'evil spirit'. And sometimes they may even call upon a local priest to perform an exorcism.

EXORCISM

The belief that evil spirits can possess a person, an object or a place has been widespread throughout the world, and the act of exorcism (from the Greek, meaning 'to drive away with an oath') is intended to force the spirit to abandon the possessed, and return to wherever it came from. What is believed to be the nature of this spirit can vary considerably: animist religions consider it a natural entity; Judaic, Christian and other major religions regard it as a member of the legion of demons who spring from the underworld; and some modern practitioners of 'alternative therapy' – such as the American psychologist Edith Fiore, author of *The Unquiet Dead* (1987) – have identified it as that of a dead person.

More specifically, exorcism is a ritual practised by Christian churches to expel demons. From the earliest Christian times, baptism was preceded by exorcism. The theory behind the practice was that the person to be baptised had been born in original sin, and, prior to accepting the Christian religion, had worshipped pagan gods – indeed, the whole world was thought to be in the power of the Devil until it was redeemed by Christ. Even in today's Christian Church the candidate for baptism, or their godparent, is required to 'renounce the Devil and all his works'.

> EXORCISM ORIGINALLY PRECEDED BAPTISM AS IT WAS BELIEVED THAT THE WHOLE WORLD WAS IN THE POWER OF THE DEVIL UNTIL IT WAS REDEEMED BY CHRIST

A possessed woman is held firmly by two men, while a priest administers the sacrament to her to exorcise an evil spirit. The spirit can be seen emerging from her mouth.

151

A Christian convert of the fourth or fifth century is exorcised by four priests before his baptism. A drawing from a contemporary bas-relief.

During the first two centuries AD, the power of exorcism was considered to be a gift that could be exercised by anyone, layman or cleric. However, around AD 250, the Church established a special class of functionaries who were named exorcists. They were only of a low order. At that time, Pope Cornelius (251–253) appointed a staff of 52, whose duties were readers, door-keepers – and exorcists, some 14 in number. Mental defectives and epileptics were believed to be troubled by the Devil, and a special part of the church was set aside for them. The job of the exorcists was to keep them quiet during the service. In this, they were more like male nurses, and very different from those who had the power to drive out demons.

DURING HER EXORCISM A YOUNG FRENCH WIDOW, ELISABETH DE RENFAING, SPOKE IN ENGLISH, FLOATED TO THE ROOF OF THE CHAPEL AND PERFORMED OTHER EXTRAORDINARY ACTS

Exorcism properly came into its own during the European witch craze of 1484–1648, when it was considered a more humane way of saving the souls of 'witches' than the customary procedure of torture, followed by committal to the fire. In 1618, for example, a young French widow on a pilgrimage to Lorraine, Elisabeth de Renfaing, accused a fellow pilgrim of trying to bewitch her. He was put to death, but Elisabeth was exorcised by two priests from the Sorbonne. According to accounts, during the exorcism she spoke in English, floated to the roof of the chapel, and performed other extraordinary acts.

(She later founded a convent in Nancy and cared for the reformed prostitutes of the city.)

The full rite of exorcism is defined in the *Rituale Romanum* of Pope Urban VIII (1623–44). A Roman Catholic priest may not perform exorcism without the authorization of his bishop, and this may be granted only to one known for his piety, prudence and moral

integrity. Signs of possession include the knowledge of matters that the subject could not have discovered by normal means, and the demonstration of abnormal strength. Urban also laid down a ritual for the exorcism of poltergeists.

Exorcism has continued into the twentieth century, both in the Roman Catholic and the Protestant churches. Fr J. de Tonquédec, who acted for the archdiocese of Paris between 1919 and 1939, wrote that more than 90 per cent of the cases he dealt with required psychiatric treatment, but he concluded that the rest were of genuine possession.

A ROMAN CATHOLIC PRIEST MAY NOT PERFORM EXORCISM WITHOUT THE AUTHORIZATION OF HIS BISHOP, AND THIS MAY BE GRANTED ONLY TO ONE KNOWN FOR HIS PIETY, PRUDENCE AND MORAL INTEGRITY

An unusual theory was put forward by the American psychologist Dr Carl Wickland, in his book *Thirty Years Among the Dead* (1924). He believed that the 'spirit' was not demonic, but merely confused, and was entrapped within the energy of the person it appeared to be afflicting. He said that he had found psychiatric persuasion to be sufficient to effect exorcism.

A recent American development of this idea is 'releasement'. Rather like a ghost, the 'possessing spirit' is usually considered to be that of a disoriented person who has died suddenly 'and is not aware that death has occurred'. The practising 'exorcist'

Particularly during the European witch hunts of 1484–1648, exorcism was considered a more humane way of saving the souls of 'witches' than consigning them to fire at the stake.

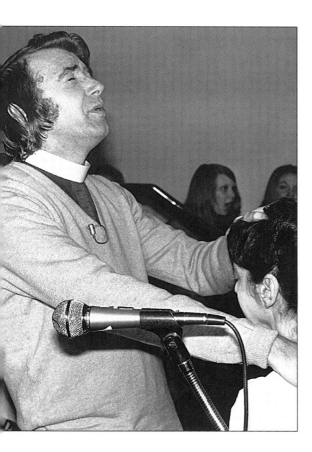

attempts to establish communication with this entity, and release it from its confused state.

In Chinese Taoist tradition, there were special rites to exorcise a 'haunted' building. The priest wore special vestments, and carried a sword made of wood, with spells carved into its blade. The sword was held over beds and other places where the unwanted spirit might dwell, and then placed upon an altar. A scroll bearing the spell of exorcism was burned, the ashes collected in a vessel filled with water, and the spirit was commanded to leave. In a final ceremony very reminiscent of Roman Catholic rites, a bunch of willow was dipped into the vessel, and the water and ashes were sprinkled about the building.

ZOMBIES

For a long time, the zombies of Haiti were considered, by sceptics, to be the subject of popular myth. Writing in 1970, anthropologist Francis Huxley remarked that 'many of the people thought to be zombies are in fact morons or idiots, of which Haiti has its fair share… Equally important, Haitians delight in telling tall

stories about things supernatural, which serve to amaze their audience and even to convince themselves, if only for a moment.'

In Haitian folklore, the zombie – a word that apparently comes from the African *nzambi*, meaning spirit of the dead – is a person who has been buried as dead, but who is resurrected by the spells of a *houngan*, a Voodoo priest, and then obeys his commands, wandering as a being without a soul. In her book *Tell My Horse* (1938), Zora Thurston gave what is now considered a classic account of a young girl from a well-to-do family who was found, four years after her burial, working as a servant in a shop; she was rescued, and placed in a French-run nunnery.

There are other stories. A Catholic priest swore to an incident in 1959, when a zombie was found wandering into the village where he had previously lived. He was taken to the police station and given salt water to drink – this is reckoned to be a sure cure for zombification. He then found his voice, and gave his name. His aunt was sent for. She said she recognized him, and declared that she had seen him buried four years earlier.

The priest arrived to interrogate the man, and was told that he was one of a large number of zombies who were controlled by a local *houngan*. Two days later the man died, and it was presumed that he had been killed by the spells

FACING PAGE: Dusted with ashes, a young Indian, said to be possessed by a demon, is escorted to the local temple for a ceremony to drive out the evil spirit.

LEFT: Though strictly limited, exorcism is still practised in the Christian Church. Here Reverend Trevor Dearing exorcises one of his congregation during a 1975 service in London.

BELOW: This Haitian woman has been transported by the hypnotic drumming and chanting of a voodoo rite.

Voodoo is still a widely held belief in Haiti, and similar practices occur in other Caribbean and South American countries, particularly in Brazil.

of the *houngan*, who did not wish his secrets to become known.

In 1980, a man who identified himself as Claidius Narcisse approached a family member in the street, and whispered his childhood nickname in her ear. There was no question that he had been buried as dead 18 years previously – his burial certificate exists to prove it.

There is a dramatic, but extremely suspect, account by W.B. Seabrook in *The Magic Island* (1935). According to this, a number of zombies were owned by a *houngan* named Joseph, and

TETRODOTOXIN, FOUND IN THE SKIN OF THE PUFFER FISH – A NORMAL INGREDIENT OF SUSHI – IS A POISON SAID TO BE 160,000 TIMES STRONGER THAN COCAINE

looked after by his wife. One day, by mistake, she gave them salted biscuits for food. Awakened from their zombie state, they made straight for the local cemetery, where they attempted to dig themselves back into their graves.

According to popular belief, the *houngan* makes use of a magic powder, which is given to a person, so that, to all intents and purposes, they have apparently died. After the burial, the *houngan* exhumes and revives the corpse, and makes it subject to his will.

Recently, investigators have obtained access to this 'magic' powder, and subjected it to analysis. They found that it contained a significant amount of the skin of the puffer fish. Species of the fish occur in the Caribbean, and also in Japanese waters. The toxin it contains is called tetrodotoxin, and it is also found in Californian newts and certain species of South American frogs. As a poison it is said to be 160,000 times stronger than cocaine. The victim of poisoning by tetrodotoxin first experiences dizziness and numbness, the blood pressure and body temperature drop, and the pulse weakens. They are likely to vomit and suffer respiratory paralysis, muscular spasms, and finally they will fall into a coma in which, apparently, death has occurred.

In Japan the flesh of the puffer fish is a normal ingredient of sushi, but it has been the cause of numerous deaths when not properly prepared. However, victims have been known to recover – in fact, those suspected of having been poisoned by puffer fish are sometimes laid by their graves for several days, in case they revive.

So it appears plausible that the tales of zombies have a basis in fact. But, some time ago, a Haitian magistrate had a different tale to tell. He gave an eyewitness account of a body being dug from its grave and re-animated. When he examined the grave the next day, he found a tube leading to the open air, so that the supposed corpse – an accomplice of the *houngan* – could continue to breathe until he was exhumed.

THE UNDEAD

Modern science fiction tales are occasionally concerned with zombie-like beings, or those who have been granted immortality. Their ancestry can be traced back to the first work in this genre, the 'Gothick' novel *Frankenstein: or The Modern Prometheus*, written by 19-year-old Mary Wollstonecraft Shelley (1797–1851), the second wife of the poet Percy Bysshe Shelley (1792–1822), which was published in 1818.

The plot of the novel – apart from the influence of the contemporary fashion for the 'Gothick' – owes something to the preoccupation of late eighteenth century anatomists and criminologists with the possibility that the 'vital spark' of an executed criminal could survive execution (see Chapter 3), and also to early experiments in the grafting of bodily parts. The story is told as a series of letters written by an English Arctic explorer named Walton.

Frankenstein is a Genevan, who discovers, while at the University of Ingoldstadt, the secret of giving life to inanimate matter. Collecting together the necessary parts of dead bodies, he assembles a being resembling a human, and brings it to life. The creature is large, and endowed with superhuman strength, but its appearance is loathsome.

Frankenstein educates his monster with the writings of Goethe, Plutarch and Milton, in order to teach it about human emotions, but as a result it becomes lonely and unhappy, and begs him to provide a female companion. When Frankenstein fails him, his creation murders his brother, a friend, and his bride Elizabeth.

The monster escapes, and Frankenstein pursues it northward into the Arctic, intending to destroy it. There he meets Walton, and tells him his story. But Frankenstein is heartbroken by the deaths of his loved ones and exhausted by his pursuit of the monster. On his deathbed, he is visited by the creature, who, once sure that Frankenstein is dead, disappears into the Arctic wastes, hoping itself to die...

The story has been adapted for film, and more than twenty 'Frankenstein' movies have so far been made – with the strange result that Frankenstein is now popularly believed to be

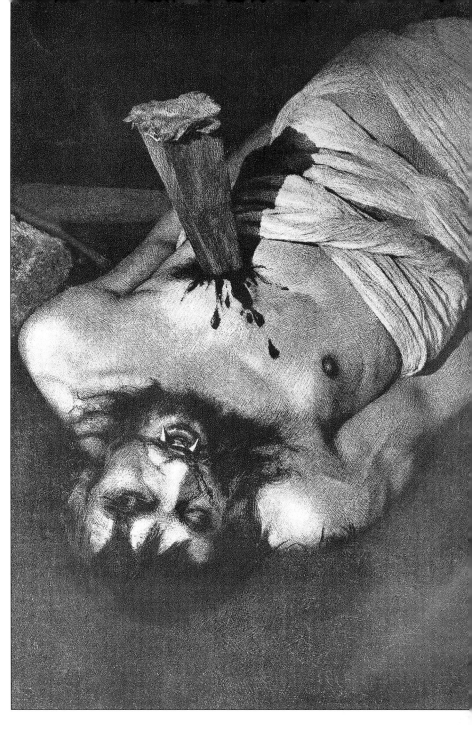

the name of the creature rather than his inventor. The first talking picture was made in 1931 by James Whale, with Boris Karloff as the monster; it was a great success, and a genre was born. The plot of the film, however, owed as much to the Jewish legend of the Golem – a clay figure brought to life by Rabbi Low to protect the Jews – as to Mary Shelley's novel.

The other great horror of nineteenth-century fiction, Dracula – the undead, has a very different history. Myths of blood-sucking monsters go back to antiquity, but accounts of the

The only sure way to dispose of a vampire: with a wooden stake driven through the heart.

157

RIGHT: Mary Wollstonecraft Shelley, whose novel **Frankenstein: or The Modern Prometheus,** *written when she was 19, introduced the Genevan doctor and his monstrous creation to the world.*

true vampires first emerged in the Balkans during the sixteenth century – the word *vampir* coming from the Magyar language. They were, perhaps, based on folk recollections of the cruelties of Vlad the Impaler and the Hungarian Countess Bathory. At first vampires were regarded as yet another form of the demons of Hell, but a seventeenth-century Greek writer named Leone Allacci made the crucial distinction that vampires were not demonic spirits, but resuscitated corpses, which relied for continuing nourishment on the blood of their victims. They are described as lean, pallid, and icy cold. When well-fed, however, they become swollen with blood like a leech, and warm to the touch. At other times, the only signs of life are their full red lips. They are characterised by long, pointed canine teeth; and may also have sharply curved fingernails, hair on the palms of their hands, and gleaming red eyes. They can call animals to do their bidding, and even change into animal shapes – but not, in the early eastern European tales, into a bat; this was a nineteenth-century addition to the mythology, after the discovery of the 'vampire bat' in South America.

AS LIVING CORPSES, VAMPIRES CAN BE ACTIVE ONLY AT NIGHT; BY DAY THEY MUST REST IN THEIR OWN GRAVES

As a living corpse, vampires can be active only at night; by day, they must rest in their own graves. There, not unlike a suicide (see Chapter 3), they can be kept from roaming by an iron or wooden stake driven through their hearts. When vampire activity was suspected in a region, the local people would examine the graves in the cemetery. They first looked for holes through which the monster could escape from its coffin and, if they found none of these, they would have to exhume the bodies in the search for one that had not decayed.

There were a number of defences against vampires, which are nowadays common knowledge among fiction-readers and most cinemagoers. The vampire shuns silver – and can be killed with a silver bullet – as well as garlic and running water, and actively fears the crucifix. But, for those who did not have these defences to hand, the creature of Balkan tradition was to be feared for a particular reason: anybody who died from loss of blood after a vampire attack was doomed to rise again as a new vampire.

The first appearance of the legend in western Europe was in 1746 when a French monk, Dom Augustin Calmet, published a learned (but credulous) treatise on the subject. The idea of the vampire appealed to the imagination of the Romantic poets, and over the next century verses were written by Goethe, Lord Byron, Southey, Gautier and Baudelaire. It appealed to the popular imagination as well: a play in Paris in the

RIGHT: The original – and most famous – portrayal of Frankenstein's monster: Boris Karloff in the 1931 film directed by James Whale. More than 20 screen adaptations of the story have followed.

1820s was soon followed by many others (including one by Alexandre Dumas), and, in 1847, by a blood-curdling 800-page bestseller, *Varney the Vampire*.

The year 1872 saw the publication of *In a Glass Darkly* by the Irish writer Sheridan Le Fanu (1814–73). This was a collection of five stories of the supernatural, purporting to be cases from the files of 'Dr Martin Hesselius, the German physician'; one, 'Carmilla', was a horrific tale of a female vampire, which was to have a powerful influence on another Irish writer, Bram Stoker (1847–1912).

Stoker's novel *Dracula* was published in 1897 – the name of the Transylvanian Count being derived from *dracul*, the Romanian for 'devil'. Just as Frankenstein is a series of letters, the story of Dracula is told in the diaries of Jonathan Harker, a young English solicitor, his fiancée Mina, her friend Lucy, and Dr John Seward, the superintendent of a lunatic asylum in Essex.

Harker, who has been summoned to Count Dracula's castle, discovers, in a ruined chapel, fifty wooden boxes filled with earth dug from the Dracula family graves, in one of which the

DURING THE 1980S, PARTLY AS

THE RESULT OF HORRIFIC

MURDERS IN CALIFORNIA, A

NUMBER OF PEOPLE CONVINCED

THEMSELVES THAT VAMPIRES

ACTUALLY EXIST

Count is lying, gorged with blood. The boxes are shipped to Whitby in Yorkshire, where Dracula escapes and vampirises Lucy.

Despite the attempts of a Professor Van Helsing – Seward's old teacher – and many blood transfusions, Lucy dies, but remains undead, until a stake is driven through her heart. The search is on to find the boxes of earth, in one of which the Count takes refuge during the day. Harker, Van Helsing and Mina trace it back to Transylvania, where they finally behead

Dracula and stab him through the heart – at which he crumbles into dust.

Like the monster of Frankenstein, Dracula has been the subject of many films, in the first of which (1931) Bela Lugosi made his name as the Count. During the 1980s, partly as the result of horrific murders in California, a number of people in America convinced themselves that vampires actually exist. The belief has been given fictional form in Brett Easton Ellis's novel *The Informers* (1994).

The ruins of Princely Court, believed to have been the home of Vlad the Impaler, at Tirgoviste, Romania.

VISIONS OF HEAVEN AND HELL

And so, what is the end? Do we expire, snuffed out like a candle? Do we linger as unhappy souls on earth, or happier souls in Summerland, endlessly awaiting spiritual fulfilment? Are we committed to a continuing circle of reincarnation? Or is there a final destination where we, retaining our personal identity, will enjoy or suffer eternal reward for our past life?

As previous chapters have shown, in most of the earliest religions – and even in some of the later developments – the afterlife had little or no place. Humankind lived, served the gods and died. Only the gods themselves lived on for ever in Heaven or the Underworld. Yet there is evidence that, even in Paleolithic times – long before the ancient Egyptians, or the writing of the *Upanishads*, long before there is any documentation of formalized religious practice – there was a belief that dead persons, or their spirits, went somewhere. The corpse was provided with

supplies for a journey; and (though much later) these might even include a chariot or a symbolic ship to travel in.

We have no way of knowing what people believed before they began to leave documentary records – inscribed clay tablets or funerary monuments – or passed on gradually garbled

FACING PAGE: The virtuous are escorted by angels to Heaven, while sinners are hurled down to eternal damnation in this fourteenth-century mural in a Romanian monastery.

LEFT: The excavation of the burial mound of the Viking queen Asa, at Oseberg in Norway, revealed the remains of a richly decorated ship, together with everything she might need on her journey to the afterlife.

161

verbal accounts from generation to generation, to be untangled during the past two centuries by anthropologists. However, the relative scarcity of the graves that have been uncovered, compared with the number of people who must have died during that time, suggests that at first only the most important were supposed to make the journey to that 'bourn from which no traveller returns'. It seems that their power on earth had raised them to a godlike status, fit to associate with the true gods.

In early times in Egypt, only the pharaohs achieved this status. Then, as the organization of the state extended, many more people – priests, government officials, merchants – had the means to make suitable provision for their

One-eyed Odin, the god who ruled over the Viking Valhalla, as represented in a medieval Danish manuscript.

burial. Indeed, it was very much as if only those who could afford the journey could hope to enjoy the afterlife. However, there appears to be little or no record of how they imagined that afterlife to be.

THE WARRIORS' HOME

In the western world, it was the Scandinavian peoples who first recorded the idea of a fully physical afterlife. One of the most elaborate Viking burials was found in Oseberg mound in southern Norway. It contained the bodies of two women (probably the ninth-century queen Asa and her maid) in a richly decorated ship, surrounded by everything they might need for their journey, including cooking utensils, beds, looms, ritual objects, a cart, sleds, thirteen horses, six dogs and two oxen. Where were they bound? To the female version of Valhalla, where they would be welcomed by Frigg, the wife of the one-eyed god Odin. Valhalla was the richest of the palaces in Asgard (one of the three domains of the Underworld), home to Odin, and to slain warriors and kings. Warriors who died on the battlefield were brought there either by Odin himself on his eight-legged horse, or by the Valkyries, his battle-maidens.

Odin held court in a vast hall glittering with gold, which had 540 doors, each wide enough to hold 800 soldiers abreast. Its walls were made up of shining spears and its roof of gleaming shields. Huge fires burnt among tables laden with food and drink. Every day, the warriors amused themselves by fighting, but were always recovered from their wounds by the evening, when they ate and drank never-ending supplies of

wild boar and horns of mead, waited on by the Valkyries. The warriors knew that one day they would be called on to fight again alongside the gods against the forces of chaos.

By contrast, most of those unfortunate enough to die a natural death, far from the battlefield, ended up in Niflheim (also known as Hel), a dismal, place of darkness and cold.

The concept of a special home for warriors was also held by the Aztecs, but here there was a significant difference. Men who had died in battle, or in ritual sacrifice in the temples, went there, because they had given their life for the nation. But women who died in childbirth were equally honoured, for the same reason. Both were clothed in beautiful garments, with

ODIN HELD COURT IN A VAST HALL GLITTERING WITH GOLD, WHICH HAD 540 DOORS, EACH WIDE ENOUGH TO HOLD 800 SOLDIERS ABREAST

gorgeous feathers in their hair, and wreathed with flowers. The warriors accompanied the sun as it rose each day, and led it to the top of the sky; the women brought it down to the western horizon, and laid it gently to sleep.

Children lost in childbirth, and those who died before they were weaned, went to the land of the milk tree, whose fruit was in the form of human breasts. People who died by drowning, or by diseases associated with water, such as dropsy, went to Tlalocan, the home of the rain god. There they found a green world, rich in butterflies, where a light rain fell constantly and everything glistened with rainbows. For the Aztecs, on their arid Mexican plateau, this paradise was perhaps the most desirable of all.

The Valkyries were the battle-maidens of Odin, who rode the storm above the fields of war, and carried back the bodies of the slain warriors to ever-lasting feasting and fighting in Valhalla. A painting by William Maud (1865-1903).

REWARDS
AND PUNISHMENTS

The name of Paradise derives from the old Persian language, and signifies a royal hunting park. In Hebrew, the word was first used in this sense in the Song of Solomon: 'A garden enclosed is my sister, my spouse; a spring shut up, a fountain sealed.'

However, the Greek version of the Hebrew scriptures used the same word to denote the earthly garden of Eden described in Genesis, and in later Jewish writings it came to mean a heavenly version of the original Eden, 'a place of rest and refreshment in which the righteous dead enjoy the glorious presence of God'. This concept was adopted by Christianity, and in

BELOW: The Aztec rain god Tlaloc, who ruled over Tlalocan, the green paradise of those who had died by drowning, or from diseases associated with water.

IN ISLAMIC PARADISE EACH MAN

IS ASSIGNED MANY BEAUTIFUL

MAIDENS, WITH EACH OF WHOM

HE MAY COHABIT ONCE FOR EVERY

DAY HE HAS FASTED IN RAMADAN

Christian art Paradise is usually represented as a beautiful garden.

In Islamic belief, the believer is welcomed into Paradise by houris. This name comes from the Arabic *hur*, which means 'the white ones', a reference to the vivid contrast of their eyes with the intense blackness of the iris, and the Koran describes them as 'virgin wives'. The dead:

recline face to face on couches adorned with gold and jewels. They shall be served with a goblet filled at a gushing fountain, which will neither dull their senses nor befuddle them; fruits as they desire, and the luscious flesh of fowls. And large-eyed houris like hidden pearls shall be their reward.

Each man is assigned many of these beautiful maidens, with each of whom he may cohabit once for every day he has fasted in Ramadan, and once for every good deed he has performed on earth.

A brief earthly vision of this paradise is said to have been accorded the members of the sect of Assassins, founded in Syria in 1090 by Hasan ibn al-Sabbah. This political terrorist movement flourished for more than two centuries, with their headquarters in the impregnable castle of Alamut. Crusaders returning to Europe called them the *hashishi*, and Marco Polo and other explorers told stories of how new recruits were drugged with hashish, and then shown a beautiful garden which, they were promised, would be their ultimate reward. The sect survives to this day as the Isma'ili sect of the Persian Shi'ites, of which the Aga Khan is the head, but there is no confirmation of these stories in any known Isma'ili text.

LEFT: Mohammed, the prophet of Islam, being carried directly to Paradise at his death.

BELOW: A recruit to the Assassin sect of Hasan ibn al-Sabbah awakens from a drugged sleep to find himself in a beautiful garden which, he was told, would be the paradise to which he would return when he died.

LEFT: *Christian belief pictured Paradise as a return to the innocence of the Garden of Eden before the Fall, as portrayed here by the Flemish painter Jan Breughel (1568–1625).*

The pains and punishments that await the infidel, or those Muslims who cannot give the correct replies to their catechism, have already been referred to in Chapter 4. Zoroastrianism seems to be the source of this concept: in both this ancient belief and Islam, the dead are envisaged as crossing a bridge, 'as narrow as a razor's edge', from which the damned tumble into Hell. In early Jewish belief, Sheol was a dark and dusty subterranean realm, where all the dead, both good and evil, were confined. Later, this idea was replaced by that of Gehenna, where only the wicked were punished, in the eternal fires. Christianity took up this concept, though whether the English word Hell is derived from the Hebrew 'Sheol', or the Norse 'Hel', is a matter of dispute.

The imagery of Heaven and Hell developed in its most comprehensive form in the Christianity of the Middle Ages, and manuscripts of the time are particularly rich in imaginative portrayals of the devilish torments that awaited the damned. The most detailed description of the medieval concept of Hell – as well as Purgatory and Paradise – is to be found in the immense epic poem, *La Divina Commedia*, written in Italian by Dante Alighieri (1265–1321). Nearly four centuries later, it greatly affected the English poet John Milton (1608–74), when he wrote *Paradise Lost*. These works, above all others, have influenced the artistic depiction of the afterlife for hundreds of years.

EASTERN BELIEFS

Both Hinduism, and the pure Buddhism that developed from it, had no conception of a physical afterlife (see Chapter 4). Those who, possibly after many reincarnations, finally achieve their salvation are absorbed, devoid of all individuality, into the pervading life-force of the cosmos.

Different forms of Buddhism, however, have developed their own mythology, the most dramatic of which is Chinese. In this belief, Heaven, ruled over by Amitabha Buddha, is accessible to all those who call upon his name and repent of their sins.

When the registers of life and death show that a man has reached the end of his earthly existence, the Lord Yama-King ('King of Death') sends his two infernal minions, Ox-head and Horse-face, to seize the man's soul and bring it before him. On reaching the underworld, the dead soul is taken before the god of walls and ditches, who interrogates him for 49 days, before handing him over to the Lord Yama-King. Sometimes the wrong soul is brought, owing to a mix-up over names or similar clerical error. In this case, it is allowed to return to earth and re-enter the body in which it lived. That is why the Chinese to this day often keep the bodies of the dead for between seven and 49 days, before burying them.

FACING PAGE: *A sixteenth-century vision of some of the torments that await the damned in Hell by the Flemish painter Pieter Huys (c.1520–84).*

The underworld has its own towns and countryside, the main town being Feng-Tu, which is entered through the large Gate of Demons. Inside are the palaces of the law courts, the places of torture, and the dwellings of functionaries, minions, and souls waiting to be re-born. This world consists of eighteen different regions, attached to ten law courts, and ruled over by ten Yama-Kings. The Lord Yama-King receives the souls of the dead, investigates their past life actions, and sends them (apart from the truly virtuous) on to the other Yama-Kings. Of these nine, eight are commissioned to punish the wicked, while the last is also entrusted with the 'wheel of transmigration', ensuring a correct fit between souls about to be reincarnated and their intended body. The second punishes dishonest intermediaries and ignorant doctors; the third, bad mandarins and forgers; the fourth, misers, dishonest traders, and blasphemers; the fifth, murderers, unbelievers, and the lustful; the sixth, the sacrilegious; the seventh, those who violated graves or ate human flesh;

BELOW: *A Tibetan bronze of the Lord Yama-King, who rules over the Buddhist underworld, receives the souls of the dead and investigates their past actions.*

the eight, those lacking filial piety; and the ninth, arson, and accidental deaths.

Not far from the town of Feng-Tu is 'the town of those who died in accidents'. Anyone who dies before their official date, as recorded in the registers of life and death, is sent there regardless of how they died. There their souls are condemned to live forever with no hope of being reborn, unless they can find a suitable replacement. After three years, they are allowed to return to their place of death and lure another to a similar end. This is why the Chinese carefully avoid visiting places of murder, suicide, or accidental death.

The Yama-Kings have thousands of minions to carry out their orders. Many varied tortures are used, often fitting the crime. Blasphemers have their tongues torn out; misers are forced to swallow molten gold; while the really wicked are plunged into boiling oil, ground in mills, or cut into little pieces.

When all the punishments have been completed, the soul is sent to the tenth Yama-King, who decides in what form it should be reborn.

Heaven, the dwelling of the gods, is divided into many levels and ruled over by the Jade Emperor. If the souls of the truly virtuous are not sent back immediately to a new life, they come to the K'un-lun mountain. There the wife of the Jade Emperor rules, from a nine-storey palace built entirely of jade, surrounded by magnificent gardens, where the peach-tree of immortality grows. Life here is a series of endless amusements and banquets.

The land of Extreme Felicity, where the Amitabha Buddha lives, is situated at the westernmost point of the universe. It is a landscape of beauty and peace, with lakes, lotus flowers, exotic birds, trees whose branches drip blossom and are decorated with wind chimes of all sizes made from precious stones and with the sound of divine voices. Those who called on Amitabha's name in their lifetime are received personally by the Buddha, who places their souls inside the lotus flowers of the lake, where they are cleansed of all impurities, before being released to mingle with the virtuous and the just.

*LEFT: **Northern European mythology has continued to inspire artists up to the present day. This illustration for Wagner's** Das Rheingold, **by Phil Redford, represents the building of the rainbow bridge between Midgard and Asgard.***

Although, in line with most religions worldwide, Chinese Buddhism has modified its beliefs in recent years, popular practices still mirror this ancient mythology. As the anthropologist M. Topley wrote in 1952, the Chinese regard the underworld:

> *rather like another China 'ploughed under', with a similar complicated system of rewards, punishments and financial obligations... Ransom payments must be made... 'squeeze' money must be given to judges, pour boire to hungry ghosts, and certificates owned... to enable one to pass any barrier encountered...*

After a funeral, these certificates are burned by the dead person's relatives, together with paper cutouts of all sorts of suitable offerings: previously they were such things as houses, sedan chairs, or even a servant, but today they are most likely to be vacuum cleaners, computers, motorcycles, credit cards, and compact-disc players.

What is so striking about these many visions of heaven and hell, in widely different cultures that had no contact with each other at the time they developed, is their similarity. Do they reflect some deep atavistic concept common to all humankind, or are they (as some would have us believe) a visionary perception of what is truly to come after death? We do not know, and only time will tell. As the English poet John Dryden (1631–1700) wrote:

> *Death in itself is nothing; but we fear*
> *To be we know not what, we know not where.*

*LEFT: **The Chinese believe that the Amitabha Buddha – the ruler of Heaven – to whom this shrine in Hangzhou is dedicated, lives in the land of Extreme Felicity, situated at the westernmost point of the universe, a landscape of beauty and peace.***

BIBLIOGRAPHY

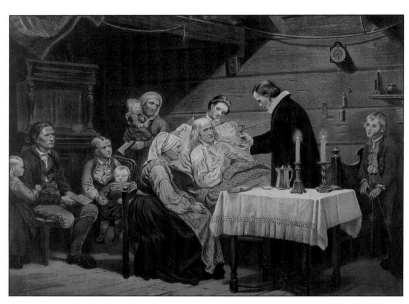

Man, Myth & Magic, ed., **Richard Cavendish**, BPC Publishing, London, 1970; eds., **Richard Cavendish and Brian Innes**, NY, 1995.

The Unexplained
Orbis Publishing, London, 1984.

Encyclopedia Britannica, 14th edition
1973 revision; CD-ROM, 1997.

Grolier Multimedia Encyclopedia, 1995

Larousse Encyclopedia of Mythology
Paul Hamlyn, London, 1959.

Phantom Encounters
Time-Life Books, Amsterdam, 1988.

Search for the Soul
Time-Life Books, Amsterdam, 1989.

The Bible

The Koran

The *Upanishads*

P.M.H. Attwater, *Beyond the Light*
Birch Lane Press, USA, 1994.

Nigel Barlay, *Dancing on the Grave*
John Murray, London, 1995.

W.H. Beable, *Epitaphs*
Simpkin Marsall, London, 1925.

John Beloff, *Parapsychology*
Athlone Press, London, 1993.

C.A. Burland, *Myths of Life & Death*
Macmillan, London, 1974.

Cottie Burland and **Werner Forman**,
Feathered Serpent and Smoking Mirror
Orbis, London, 1975.

Richard Cavendish, ed., *Mythology: An Illustrated Encyclopedia*
Orbis Publishing, London, 1980.

Richard Cavendish, *The Black Arts*
Routledge & Kegan Paul, London, 1967.

Daniel Cohen, *Encyclopedia of Ghosts*
Michael O'Mara Books, London, 1994.

Arthur Cotterell, *The Illustrated Encyclopedia of Myths & Legends*
Guild Publishing, London, 1989.

J.S. Curl, *A Celebration of Death*
Batsford, London, 1993.

Mike Dash, *Borderlands*
William Heinemann, London, 1997.

Claude Gagnière, *Des Mots et Merveilles*
Robert Laffont, Paris, 1994.

Sue Gill and **John Fox,** *The Dead Good Funerals Book*
Engineers of the Imagination, Ulverston, 1996.

Rosemary Goring, ed., *Chambers Dictionary of Beliefs and Religions*
W. & R. Chambers, Edinburgh, 1992.

Rosemary Ellen Guiley, *Encyclopedia of Mystical & Paranormal Experience*
Harper, San Francisco, 1991.

Brian Innes, *The Catalogue of Ghost Sightings*
Blandford, London, 1996.

Jeffrey Iverson, *In Search of the Dead*
BBC Books, London, 1992.

Robert Kastenbaum, *Is There Life After Death?*
Prion, London, 1995.

Thomas A. Kselman, *Death and the Afterlife in Modern France*
Princeton University Press, 1993.

Elisabeth Kübler-Ross, *Questions and Answers on Death and Dying*
Macmillan, New York,1974.

Elisabeth Kübler-Ross, *Death: The Final Stages of Growth*
Prentice-Hall, Englewood Cliffs, New Jersey, 1975.

James R. Lewis, *Encyclopedia of Afterlife Beliefs and Phenomena*
Visible Ink, Detroit, 1995.

Filippo Liverziani, *Life, Death & Consciousness*
Prism Press, Bridport, 1991.

Magnus Magnusson, *Hammer of the North*
Orbis, London, 1976.

Cedric Mimms, *When We Die*
Robinson, London, 1998.

David Wendell Moller, *Confronting Death*
Oxford University Press, New York, 1996.

Peter Moss, *Encounters with the Past*
Sidgwick & Jackson, London, 1979.

Anthony North, *The Paranormal*
Blandford, London, 1996.

Jenny Paschall & **Ron Lyon,** *Hatches, Matches & Dispatches*
HarperCollins, London, 1997.

Christine Quigley, *The Corpse: A History*
McFarland, Jefferson NC, 1996.

Philip Reder, *Epitaphs*
Michael Joseph, London, 1969.

Archie E. Roy, *A Sense of Something Strange*
Dog & Bone, Glasgow, 1990.

Marisa St Clair, *Near-Death Experience*
Blandford, London, 1998.

John and Anne Spencer, *The Encyclopedia of Ghosts and Spirits*
Headline, London, 1992.

Roy Stemman, *Reincarnation*
Piatkus, London, 1997.

Reuben Stone, *Life After Death*
Blitz Editions, London, 1993.

Allen Troy, *Disaster*
publisher unknown, 1974.

Terry White, *The Sceptical Occultist*
Arrow Books, London, 1995.

D.M. Wilson, *Awful Ends*
British Museum Press, London, 1992.

Ian Wilson, *In Search of Ghosts*
Headline, London, 1995.

Ian Wilson, *Life After Death*
Sidgwick & Jackson, London, 1997.

INDEX

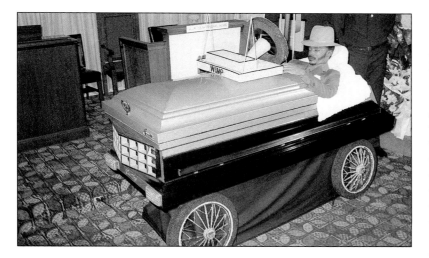

PICTURE CREDITS

KEY: l–left, r–right, t–top, b–bottom

Cover: E.T. Archive (background); **Nicolas Sapieha; Kea Publishing Services/Corbis** (insert)

Aerofilms: 88b; **AFP/EPA Photo/Joseph Barrak/JU**: 21; **AKG, London**: 96, 161, Erich Lessing 167; **Archivo Iconografico, S. A., Barcelona**: 103t, 152-3; **Associated Press/Sydney Morning Herald**: 49; **The Bridgeman Art Library, London/ New York**: *Ascent of the Prophet Muhammad to Heaven*, by Aqa Mirak, 16th century, Persian, British Library 104-5, *The Resurrection of Lazarus* (vellum) by Pol de Limbourg/Tres Riches Heures du Duc de Berry, early 15th century, Musee Conde, Chantilly /Roger-Viollet 106, *The Weighing of the Heart against Maat's Feather of Truth* from The Book of the Dead of the Royal Scribe Hunefer, British Museum, London 108-9, *Panel of the Descent into Limbo* from the altarpiece of the Convent of Santo Sepulchro, Zaragoza by Jaume Serra, Museo Provincial de Bellas Artes, Zaragoza, Spain/Index 109t, *Snakes and Ladders* - the path to heaven or hell, mid-18th century, Victoria & Albert Museum, London 111b, *Odin: the Norse god, with his two crows, Hugin (thought) and Munin (memory)*, Royal Library, Copenhagen, Denmark 162, *The Ride of the Valkyries* by William T. Maud, Gavin Graham Gallery, London 163, *Donner and Froh Create the Rainbow Bridge for the Gods to Cross to Valhalla*, illustration for 'Das Rheingold' (linocut) by Phil Redford (living artist), Private Collection 169t; **Colorific**: 51; **Corbis**: Nicolas Sapieha; Kea Publishing Services 3, Corbis-Bettmann 5, Historical Picture Archive 6, Arte & Immagini SRL 7, Corbis-Bettmann 8 and 9, David Lees 10, Francis G. Mayer 11, Nicolas Sapieha, Kea Publishing Services 12, Robert Pickett

13, Corbis-Bettmann 14, Nevada Wier 15, Roger Ressmeyer 16b, Vittoriano Rastelli 17, Jan Butchofsky-Houser 18l, Tim Page 18r, Paul A. Souders 19, Jack Moebes 22, Robert Maass 23, Corbis-Bettmann 24, North Carolina Museum of Art 26r, W. Perry Conway 27, Albrecht G. Schaefer 30, Chris Rainier 31, Mimmo Jodice 34-35, UPI/Corbis-Bettmann 36, National Archives 37, Historical Picture Archive 38, UPI/Corbis-Bettmann 39b/t, Library of Congress 40b, Hulton-Deutsch Collection 40-41, UPI/Corbis-Bettmann 42t, Asian Art & Archeology, Inc. 42b, Melvyn P. Lawes; Papilio 43t, Bob Rowan; Progressive Image 43b, UPI/Corbis-Bettmann 44b, Chris Hellier 45b, National Institutes of Health 47t, Corbis-Bettmann 47b, Hulton-Deutsch Collection 55b, Corbis-Bettmann 55t and 56-7, Alison Wright 58, Weegee/ UPI/corbis-Bettmann 60t, Todd Gipstein 60b, UPI/Corbis-Bettmann 61b/173, Bojan Brecelj 62tr, Corbis 62l, Owen Franken 63, Albrecht G. Schaefer 64t, Lindsay Hebberd 66t, Nathan Benn 66b/171b, Miki Kratsman 67t/174, Earl Kowall 67b, Barry Lewis 68, Paul Almasy 69/171t, Hulton-Deutsch Collection 70t, Patrick Field; Eye Ubiquitous 70b, Jim Sugar Photography 71,

Corbis-Bettmann 72t, Macduff Everton 74, Corbis-Bettmann 76-7 and 77, Charles & Josette Lenars 78 and 79, Michael Nicholson 80l, Robert Estall 80r, Corbis 81r, Gianni Dagli Orti 81l, Yann Arthus-Bertrand 82l, Richard T. Nowitz 82r, Owen Franken 83b, Reinhard Eisele 83t, Chris Hellier 84t/176, Jerry Cooke 84b, Jack Fields 85b/172, Angelo Hornak 85t, Corbis-Bettmann 86r, Hulton-Deutsch Collection 86l and 87, Catherine Karnow 88t, Steve Raymer 89, Hulton-Deutsch Collection 90, Joseph Sohm; ChromoSohm Inc. 91/ 175, Angelo Hornak 92t, Michael St. Maur Sheil 92-3, Earl Kowall 94, Charles & Josette Lenars 95b, Mimmo Jodice 99, Luca I. Tettoni 101, Michael Freeman 102t, Seattle Art Museum 102-3, Corbis-Bettmann 104b, Lindsay Hebberd 105b, Corbis-Bettmann 107, Paul Almasy 110, Adam Woolfitt 111t, Charles & Josette Lenars 112, Chris Rainier 113, Julia Waterlow; Eye Ubiquitous 115b, UPI/Corbis-Bettmann 115t, Michael Nicholson 118t, Hulton-Deutsch Collection 118b, Corbis-Bettmann 119b, Hulton-Deutsch Collection 120b and 122, Kimbell Art Museum 124-5 and 124b, Daniel Laine 125b, Michael Maslan Historic Photographs, Christel Gerstenberg

128, Corbis 129, Historical Picture Archive 134-5, Gianni Dagli Orti 136-7, Corbis-Bettmann 138, Hulton-Deutsch Collection 139, Corbis-Bettmann 140, UPI/ Corbis -Bettmann 141, Earl Kowall 143, Caroline Penn 146b, Corbis-Bettmann 149, Hulton-Deutsch Collection 150t, National Institutes of Health 151, Sheldan Collins 154, Hulton-Deutsch Collection 155t, Bradley Smith 155b, Hulton-Deutsch Collection 156, Corbis-Bettmann 157, 158 t/b, Janet Wishnetsky 159, Gianni Dagli Orti 166, Nazima Kowall 169b, Paul Almasy 171t, Nathan Benn 171b, Jack Fields 172, UPI/Corbis-Bettmann 173, Miki Kratsman 174, Joseph Sohm; ChromoSohm Inc. 175, Chris Hellier 176; **E. T. Archive**: British Library 98, Tate Gallery 133, E. T. Archive 160, Anthropological Museum Mexico 164; **Mary Evans Picture Library**: 32, 33, 54, 61t/170, 72b, 117, 148, 164-5, 165, Lawrie Berger 150b; **Evans Universal, Leeds**: 73; **Werner Forman Archive**: Topkapi Palace Museum, Istanbul 59, Egyptian Museum, Cairo 64br; 65, 100, Philip Goldman Collection 168; **Fortean Picture Library**: Larry E. Arnold 52-3; 119t, 121, 126b, 130, Tony O'Rahilly 142; 144, Joanne Crowther 145; 152t; **Hulton Getty Picture Collection**: 123t; **The Hutchison Library**: Sarah Errington 26l; **The Image Bank**: P. McConville 97, Stephen Marks 131; Reproduced by permission of the **Marquess of Bath, Longleat House** 146t; **Peter Newark's Western Americana**: 28/9, 29b, 114b, 114t; **Rex Features**: David McNew/Sipa Press 44-5, Rick Colls 95t; **Science Photo Library**: BSIP, ABELES 16t, BSIP, LECA 46; **Frank Spooner Pictures**: Pugliano/Liaison/ Gamma 48, Sander/Gamma Liaison 137t; **Topham Picturepoint**: 126t, 132.